Experiencing and Overcoming Schizoaffective Disorder

A Memoir

By: Steve Colori

For a patient to be diagnosed with schizoaffective disorder, he or she must have all the symptoms of schizophrenia and all the symptoms of bipolar disorder simultaneously.

This memoir is a recollection and analysis of my life experiences that pertain to the causes, experience, and overcoming of schizoaffective disorder. For the most part I have had a very positive life and have experienced many enjoyable times and wouldn't want anyone to think otherwise. This book is dedicated to my family, doctor, and friends who were crucial in my recovery and my development beyond recovery. They mean the world to me.

Citations

The contents of the following articles are within this text and were written by Steve Colori.

Colori, S: Autobibliotherapy. Schizophrenia Bulletin. First published online: 2015 February; doi: 10/1093/schbul/sbv004

Colori, S : Exposure Therapy. Schizophrenia Bulletin. First published online: 2015 April : doi: 10.1093/schbul/sbv049

Colori, S: Journaling as Therapy. Schizophrenia Bulletin. First published online 2015 May : 10.1093/schbul/sbv066

Colori, S : The Importance of Talk Therapy. Schizophrenia Bulletin. First published online: 2014 June; doi: 10.1093/schbul/sbu091

Colori, S: Understanding Referential Thinking. Schizophrenia Bulletin. First published online : 2015 February ; doi: 10.1093/schbul/sbv005

Table of Contents

Chapter 1
Growing Up with
Cognitive Impairment

When I was in 3rd grade, I learned that I was chemically imbalanced and I had no idea what this meant. I was worried because I knew something was wrong but I wasn't quite sure what. I decided to completely ignore this information although it sat in the back of my mind whenever I was having any social difficulty throughout my life. I felt somewhat inadequate as a result of thinking I had a deficiency and I thought there must be something biologically wrong with me which was causing my social ineptitude. I did well in school but I never sat still and I was talkative to the point where teachers asked for quietness multiple times per class. My parents and other adults frequently commented on my restlessness; at the end of the day I occasionally fell asleep in the middle of speaking a sentence. I was always moving and they thought I had ADHD but I wasn't medicated for it. I frequently had trouble paying attention while in conversation. There were times when I looked directly at whoever was speaking, straining to process the words, but my conscious mind was unable to make any sense of the information being conveyed. It felt as though a cloud filled my consciousness during these times and there was no space left in which to process anything. The cloud blocked the space where conscious thought should have occurred and also blocked my mental receptiveness. I would ask the speaker to repeat himself, and he would, but even then I struggled to gain any information.

While communicating, I experienced thought

blocking and racing thoughts periodically. During conversations I sometimes consciously decided to respond to the person who was talking to me but I couldn't put together an intelligent answer; many times I barely said anything at all. I experienced *racing thoughts*, an overload of too many thoughts, each successively flashing into my mind. Each thought was momentarily visible but quickly replaced by a different one, which left me unable to take hold of any of these thoughts, make sense of them, and/or turn them into something useful. The experience is similar to a video passing by too quickly. This inhibited my ability to speak. I was sometimes able to give a short response of several words at most but I didn't have the processing capacity for extensive conversation while this was occurring.

I also had *thought blocking,* which came in several forms. Sometimes it felt as though multiple thoughts were crammed into my mind simultaneously and there were so many ideas cueing at once that it seemed impossible to choose the one I wanted. At other times, it seemed like there was a physical impediment denying me access to the language-processing function of my mind. I just drew complete blanks and all the thoughts that were in my mind simply vacated the premises. I knew deep down that everyone else could process everything they were hearing and that they could communicate effectively and I always wondered why I had this impediment. I felt disadvantaged and couldn't figure out why I would be created any differently than anyone else. I attributed it to being chemically imbalanced, but I kept this to myself. I told people I had ADD.

My acceptance of having some sort of mental inhibition as an inherent personality trait only fostered more racing thoughts and thought blocking because I became inclined to allow them to happen instead of working through them. When I currently encounter racing thoughts and thought blocking I work to slow my thoughts down and allow them to flow. I found thought blocking has also been a result of social factors. Sometimes a momentary fear that I am about to express myself in a weird or inappropriate way will lead to thought blocking. To counter this, I'll add extra pauses in my speech. I may also use extra words before saying the words I originally thought might be expressed in a socially unacceptable way. This allows me to either search for different words or change the way I want to deliver the message; it gives me time to adjust my tone of voice or the level of emotion with which I express the thought.

Another, more common communication problem I've had to learn to manage is not being able to find the exact word I am looking for. The words are either on the tip of my tongue or just out of reach. I have found there are many ways to express an idea and I'll simply express my thoughts with a different set of words. This has happened to me when there is a socially common term or idiom with which everyone is familiar and I'm unable to access it. I've learned to just put it in my own terms. The same message is brought across, and often my terms are more descriptive of the concept I'm trying to express because they are more specific to the situation and idea I am trying to talk about.

My communication difficulties led people to believe I was dumb, but I was really quite intelligent. My processing and speaking troubles usually only occurred in social situations. In class I was able to pay better attention. When I focused, my school work was excellent, but I frequently made small mistakes as a result of rushing. I usually enjoyed tests and quizzes because I had a sharp memory and it was easier to focus on a paper I could reread—unlike when I was socializing, I could erase my mistakes. In high school I achieved a 3.66 GPA with little to no studying, which proves that having a communication disorder does not mean someone is unintelligent. Although I could be spacey at times, I was also able to hyper-focus periodically when necessary. During these times my thinking was lucid and my energy level was higher. I was in an elevated state of mind where the task at hand was all that registered in my consciousness. Everything made much better sense and my processing abilities were enhanced. I was able to complete my work rather quickly; I was almost always one of the first students taking a test.

I grew up in a rural town with a population of approximately 7,000 residents and the biggest news for my group of friends was usually the sports scores. Everyone knew each other's business; I saw the same people every day.

I broke my arm the summer after 6th grade. Unable to participate in sports, I fell into a severe depression. My friends wanted to play outside but I was unable to interact because of my broken arm and I chose to stay home alone. My depression gradually got worse and, after a couple months of seclusion, I became estranged from my peers. I was losing my socialization skills and I was unable to connect with anyone.

My depression became a cycle; I expressed negativity which in turn created more situations which led to more negative emotions. I habitually complained and constantly searched for—and found—negativity in everything.

When people are feeling negative it makes the people around them unhappy. When I was in bad moods I gave voice to negative opinions and beliefs. I focused on negative occurrences from my surroundings. I caused the people around me to share my negativity in the attempt to be as agreeable as they could be

—out of courtesy. Our most recent thoughts reverberate in our subconscious and after a while it was difficult for me to eliminate negativity because that was the only thing I had been expressing and hearing. Young people enjoy finding themselves in agreement, which results in kids adopting the same beliefs, moods, mannerisms, and habits as the people they interact with. People adopt the moods and behaviors of their peers because they think it will help them fit in better.

Often, positive people are positive because they're surrounded with positive influences, many times by choice and sometimes by chance. When I have kept a positive attitude, people have expected a positive conversation before speaking with me and they have brought a better attitude to the conversation. When I was constantly negative people expected negativity before even interacting with me. This gave them a negative perception of me and made them more negative when we interacted.

Once school started again I was constantly ridiculed. I sat with the same few people every day at lunch and I tried fitting in but they only kept me around to make fun of me. They constantly picked out everything I did wrong, and my fear of being ridiculed only resulted in me making more outlandish comments which were then further ridiculed. I also lacked the intellect to defend myself. Sometimes my classmates made derisive comments and I tried to think of something to say but before I could defend myself they continued on. Other times there were brief moments when I could have responded but I was usually too afraid to do so. They continued until they were laughing with their friends and at this point it seemed pointless to respond at all. I was also suppressed by my own negative mentality. I believed that if I did say anything to defend myself something bad would result from it. The very few times I did stand up for myself the disparager usually made a sharp authoritative comment to try to put me back down; unfortunately, this usually worked. This only compelled people to pick on me more because I was someone they could release their frustrations on, or use to boost their self-esteem, without receiving any punishment for doing so. In short, I was an easy target. My bullies thought they were better than I was and built their self-esteem upon this notion. It would have been an insult for me to get the better of any of them and they strove to ensure this didn't happen.

Sometimes students told me I should kill myself and there was one girl in particular who stated this several times a day. Even in class no one wanted to work with me or even be anywhere near me because they were afraid other students would think that they weren't cool because they had been associating with me. I became fairly eccentric and my sense of humor was skewed because I had been so alienated from healthy socialization. I sometimes told jokes that didn't make any sense and people took the opportunity to make fun of me.

Some days I tried keeping a good humor about the teasing, attempting to get along with the group, but this only contributed to my despair and the decimation of my self-esteem. Their "humor" was disparaging, not friendly. My acceptance of their joking and ridicule supported *their belief* that they could say whatever they wanted about me, that what they were saying was acceptable and true. It also made me feel I deserved it in some way. Although I was different and sometimes a bit perturbing, I meant no one any harm and certainly didn't deserve what I was getting. Sometimes students played practical jokes on me and I was so eager just to interact with others that I partially went along with the jokes. I was hoping that I could connect better with my peers but this only fueled the fire.

The ridiculing let up inside the classroom because students were afraid teachers would discipline them, but in the hallways and the lunchroom it was frequent and difficult to bare. This made me really enjoy the comfort of the classroom and dread every other place.

After a while I became so accustomed to negativity that I yearned for it because I was so used to experiencing it; there was a certain comfort level with feeling emotions I was familiar with. I still maintained good grades, partially because I was so interested in taking my mind off everything else happening in my life, and also because I had been taught that school was important.

Once I was home from school I stayed in my room or in the basement, in complete isolation. Being with people was a painful experience so I sought the comfort of solitude. Although solitude was also fairly painful, I developed a certain comfort level watching TV and playing video games alone. It felt better than being with people who were going to make fun of me. I also lost my appetite and became fairly skinny.

One night in 7th grade, after a difficult day at school I had a nervous breakdown. I started uncontrollably shaking, crying, and hyperventilating. I completely lost control of my body and my nerves were shot. After it happened I felt almost relieved and restored to a neutral emotional state which I hadn't experienced in months. I had been so negative about absolutely everything in my life that my body couldn't take it anymore and this breakdown was triggered. I wanted to attend another school but my parents thought the one in my small town would provide a better education and convinced me to stay.

My depression got to a point where I picked up a knife in the middle of the night and nearly committed suicide, but I decided against it and went back to the comfort of my bed. A few days after this I decided I needed some help. I reached out to a classmate and told him about my experience with the knife. After that I think he told everyone to be easier on me and everyone was much kinder.

I started playing sports again in the spring of 7th grade and this helped my mood. I was with people every day after school and I was exercising and regaining my physical strength. I was getting along better with friends because we were talking sports and we were constantly together during practice. Baseball was one of my favorite sports growing up, and just being on the field created comfort and happiness for me. I had many positive memories associated with the sport from having practiced with my Dad and having played with my friends for most of my life. I recommend that anyone in a depression to get back to the activities that have created the most happiness. Those enjoyable activities can trigger positive memories and really improve your emotional state, which is what baseball did for me. As the year progressed I improved I played better; I received the award for Most Improved Player at our baseball banquet.

Towards the end of 7th grade, people still picked on me but I was beginning to stand up for myself. Although I still wasn't mentally equipped to verbally defend myself, I actually wound up fighting a kid in the school yard after he made some negative comments about me. It was the end of the day. He had a lot to say and I took my usual approach of not saying anything. He started calling me chicken and that was it. He said he could whip me but I was pretty strong from my sports and he was a bit of a runt. We went out to the field and had it out. Although fighting is an awful thing and should be avoided, least I stood up for myself and everyone knew about it. People began thinking I would stand up for myself and started picking on me less. I recommend for anyone being picked on to have the courage to stand up for yourself, because you need to let people know they can't make fun of you and make you the butt of their jokes. This can be extremely difficult at first and takes tremendous effort and courage, but the more you stand up for yourself the easier it becomes. Even if you only make a small comment in your defense, bullies will realize you're not an easy target. You'll be seen as someone who is worthy of respect, because you have demonstrated self-respect by standing up for yourself.

Now that I'm older I usually don't have to stand up for myself, but when I do, I make a point to not make the situation awkward. I'll respond with a joking remark which indicates I'm not really happy with what someone is saying. It's also important to discern between friendly joking and disparaging joking because friendly joking is sometimes essential to connecting with friends.

In high school, I played football and baseball and would have considered myself not so much a "student-athlete" as an "athlete-student," because I placed all my emphasis on sports. I still completed my school work exceptionally with very little effort. My general attire in school was a baseball hat with sweat pants and a t-shirt. If I felt like dressing up I'd wear basketball shorts and a polo shirt, and I always accompanied my outfits with running shoes. I trained for sports regularly and went to the gym two or three times a week as well as running 4-6 miles three times a week on top of practices.

All of this physical activity may have been part of the reason for my "spaciness;" some of it was exhaustion and some of it was cognitive impairment. I was picked on jokingly for being less aware and intelligent than my classmates. I participated in the creation of my "spacy" image through my willingness to go along with other peoples' perception of me. I let them think I was dumb. I laughed at my own expense. I thought if I went along with people's joking they would like me more. My middle school experience had created a tremendous fear of loneliness and I constantly sought others' approval.

At times I assumed a cocky attitude, which was a facade for my diffidence. I usually didn't stand up for myself because I lacked the courage and the wit. Occasionally I myself picked on people who I thought were easy targets to boost my own self-esteem. I was also fairly passive from having watched too much television. The combination of ridicule, passivity, and lack of mental clarity created an overwhelming feeling of mental inhibition and lack of control over my life.

There was a two month spurt interval where I took Concerta to stabilize my thinking and there were drastic improvements in my stream of consciousness. Before taking Concerta I had many racing thoughts. I had never experienced a clear stream of consciousness where I was fluidly articulating my thoughts and consciously thinking my way through situations. My mind felt like a crammed space in which it was difficult to maneuver. My conversations completely changed with Concerta because I was able to consciously process verbal communication and my attentiveness was excellent. I had more to say and could pinpoint my thoughts and directly respond to people's questions. My attentiveness in the classroom also improved and my grades changed from B's and A's to all A's without my putting in any extra work. With Concerta my mind felt spacious, and this was relaxing. The thought blocking went away and racing thoughts were completely elimi-nated. My social life was also improving and people hardly made fun of me because my interactions were more intelligent and I was able to better process the words I was hearing. Concerta had a calming effect and it slowed everything down for me. My speech was even a little slower and my energy level had decreased a bit too. I took my time walking from place to place and never felt a need to rush to get anywhere. I had previ-ously rushed to places, mostly because of my high-en-ergy levels, but also because I never felt comfortable being in the place I was in.

Baseball season was approaching. I was taking Concerta during the off season but I decided my athlet-ics would suffer if I continued taking it. I thought I would need the energy which Concerta took from me and would be less competitive without it. I also wanted to succeed by my own merit rather than with the help of any "performance enhancing" drugs. So I decided to stop taking the medication. At the time I didn't realize I was already at a disadvantage without the medication and it was merely leveling the playing field.

Although I did have a regular group of friends I hung out with I never felt right, due to people still mak-ing fun of me. This usually made me feel as though I had done something wrong. I did make some mistakes, as we all do, growing up. But my mistakes were exag-gerated by others who were looking for reasons to scold someone. I was constantly made the scape-goat for everything and anything that went wrong. Even when I had nothing to do with the problem, people blamed me anyways because they thought it was hu-morous. They also thought it was easier than taking the responsibility themselves. People always told me they were better than I was, too. I was one of the less re-spected guys in the group; sometimes people didn't wait up for me when we walked from place to place. Occurrences of this nature were regular and painfull wanted confidence and meaning in my life but I didn't possess the wherewithal to make sound decisions. I was completely unaware of how to obtain the things I wanted out of life, which were things I couldn't consciously define.

My friends and I were always sarcastic —nothing meaningful meant anything to us. My life was one punch-line after another and I didn't know how to find relevance. I had an incredible amount of energy but I was still unable to sustain any substantive thoughts. I also wasn't a reader at the time and this definitely contributed to my lack of intellect.

I prioritized popularity as my number one goal mostly because of the distress of my middle school experience. I adopted my values to fit main stream culture as a means to fit in. Inwardly we all knew these values were wrong but they were constantly reinforced by most of our influences and this was persuasive. We misunderstand much of what we were hearing and watching. We thought there must be righteousness in these ideas that were all over the radio and the television. The values expressed in the media crept into our way of relating to one another. When adults were around, we said what they probably wanted to hear, but on our own we believed in basically anything that sounded appealing to us at the time.

Developing Schizoaffective Disorder

Mulling over which college to attend, I decided to go somewhere I could meet new people and hopefully find a group of friends who were kind to me and appreciated me. I was the captain of the football team in my senior year, was all-league, and had received division two football scholarships and other offers, but decided I didn't want to continue playing. I went to an out of state school knowing I was one of the few from my graduating class who had applied there. It was one of the best schools I was accepted to. Also, it was a large university and if I wanted to switch my major from business to something else I'd have many options. I wound up making new friends and really enjoyed my freshman year. I spent three or four nights a week drinking while managing to maintain a 3.0 GPA. It was a wild year. My entire life was structured around drinking and I was constantly thinking and joking about alcohol and partying with friends.

During this year, my two best friends decided to join a fraternity. I was at a loss for who I'd hang out with when they surrounded themselves with their new "brothers". I began to hang out with people I barely knew; I missed my old friends. We still hung out occasionally but most of their time was consumed by pledging.

Freshman year lacked academic rigor; it left me too much free time, which I spent it watching television and wasting away. I could feel my mind becoming increasingly duller, and life felt increasingly meaningless without friends or much work to do. For a while I contemplated taking steroids, but I was afraid of the side effects. Some acquaintances found a muscle building energy drink which was FDA approved, so I decided to join them in drinking it—because of the FDA approval. I took this nitrogen- based drink on a regular basis, hoping I would develop more muscle and be more attractive. At the time I valued aesthetics, and with the bodily improvements the drink provided, my confidence and self-esteem improved. Physically the drink provided an abundance of B vitamins and caffeine which made me happier. I was already a high- energy person and the caffeine helped me push the limits of my wakefulness. I could go weeks on four or five hours of sleep without feeling any negative effects from sleep deprivation.

This continued into the summer when I obtained a job working on a grounds crew at a ballpark, which required working sixteen-hour days for ten day stretches. During the home stretches we worked 110 hours and while the team was away we worked thirty. The employer had a two week pay period and would divide the total hours amongst both weeks, so the time cards looked as though employees had worked 140 hours in two weeks, which totaled 70 hours per week and was still under the legal labor limit.

The one type of work I enjoyed more than any other was manual labor, which had to do with my high-energy levels. I was very diligent because I had the energy but also because I associated manual labor with athletics, always a source of happiness for me. After putting forth a good day's work I usually felt pretty good about myself. This meaningful feeling was what I had lacked during my freshman year of college. I liked how I felt, and as a result I worked as many hours as I possibly could. Keeping balance in my life would have been great for me but I was convinced of the positive effects that working hard and not complaining would have on my well-being and emotional health.

Sometimes you need to work overtime but rest and fun activities are definitely a necessity as well. (It's also all right to complain once in a while.) I was in a positive environment and enjoyed the people I was with, so I didn't think much of it at the time. My processing speed definitely decreased immensely and I was starting to allow thoughts I would once deem ridiculous to enter my belief system. I still felt good from working so I continued with my rigorous weeks. I used my nitrogen muscle building energy drink to meet my high energy demands during the 110 hour weeks. During the 30 hour weeks, I was busy between work, my friends, the gym, and other fun times, and I was beginning to become a bit overtired. I was learning how to push my limits during the ten day stretches and realized I didn't need nearly as much sleep as I previously thought I did.

My place of employment was located in the heart of a tough city, and the people I met constantly talked about the difficulty of living there. They were also genuine and truly conscientious of those in their circle and their values started resonating with me. I was adopting their speech mannerisms and wanted to feel I belonged. Their lives sounded meaningful, which is how I wanted mine to be. They talked about the gun shots they heard at night and how people were shot every day where they lived. One recalled a moment when he watched someone get shot and killed from a hundred feet away. I began to associate meaningfulness with enduring adversity. I was motivated to make my life as difficult as it could be. I hadn't thought much about how adversity factors into well-being and the type of adversity I wanted or needed in my life. Adversity isn't always good, especially when it is detrimental to one's health.

The beginning of the next school year arrived and I was excited to return. One of my best friends at the time also kept a busy schedule and we started talking about how we could still be perfectly functional with only four hours of sleep. I really believed that if other people —such as military personnel—could go on four hours of sleep, then I definitely could too. And there was no reason not to! What I didn't realize was after they do this for a while they return to a regular sleeping schedule and catch up on their sleep. My friends and I talked about over-tiredness as if it were a badge of honor. But being tired is difficult. I felt invincible because everything in my life was going well. I ignored signs of deteriorating health. I also didn't want to sleep because my life was very enjoyable at the time.

In some cases it's perfectly acceptable to believe you can do what you set your mind to, but science can't be ignored. The human body has limits and optimal functioning conditions, and if these are ignored it can be extremely detrimental. The difficulty of my school work increased and my grades began to slip drastically. I wasn't up for the academic challenge my sophomore year brought.

I was also becoming contentious and nearly fought a couple of people over trivial matters. One person jokingly stated that I wasn't going to pass a class. Whether I not I would pass was in fact an issue at the time, but I should have brushed his remark aside in good humor. Instead I got in his face and made a rude comment and created a problem over something that could have been easily ignored. Occurrences like this were happening periodically, when in the past they never had.

I intentionally ignored and avoided the people I grew up with because their ridicule and negativity towards me outweighed any good times we had ever had. I only wanted to remember the bad things, not realizing that every group of friends disparages one another when they are young. Although they were probably changing and becoming nicer people, I was unable to see. I remembered their high school personalities rather than getting to know them for who they had become.

I was living alone for the first time in my life and

felt a new personal freedom. I was in charge and I was responsible for all my decisions and this felt pretty good. I started slipping from the values my parents had instilled in me, and started adopting the values of those around me. During high school, we only talked about going against our values; we usually ended up making the right decisions. But this changed in college. For me, college was a strange place where immature values ran rampant and were commonly accepted, because the only authorities on social well-being were the students. My gait changed and I walked arrogantly as if every step was some act of defiance. People would make jokes in good humor and I would take offense, thinking I was too good to allow anyone to make fun of me. I changed my regular speech to a slang which reflected that of rappers. I intentionally tried to sound less intelligent, which I thought would make me more popular. I used words like "yo" constantly and never put a g on the end of -ing words. I always tried to keep a cool countenance which suggested I knew something about life other people didn't. I began thinking that fighting was good and you had to fight in order to stand up for yourself, when in reality it's easier, better, and smarter to avoid any trouble by being kind and intelligent. I constantly went to the gym believing I needed musculature to impress people. During the previous summer, when I started filling out with muscle, I had bought different clothes which I thought were more stylish. I liked baggy t-shirts with cursive writing, jeans that were ripped, white sneakers with white laces, and I always gelled my hair. I was completely immersed in sensory perceptions and thought I was really convincing people of my "coolness." In reality I was making a fool of myself.

If I'd had any bit of introspection, I would have been able to easily determine that there were negative changes in my demeanor. I was on a bad path. Unfortunately, I lacked the humility to admit I had any faults. I was afraid of admitting I had faults because I thought if I did have them it would make me subhuman, so I ignored them and acted as though everything was fine. In my group of friends it wasn't acceptable to have any real difficulties. Being "cool" and being a man meant enduring your problems instead of thinking them through or talking with someone about them and fixing them. I wasn't much of a problem solver and people usually didn't ask me for personal advice, so I had the impression that most people led perfect lives. The truth is the exact opposite: most people have issues but just don't discuss them publicly. At this age, I felt it was a badge of honor to have problems, that having a hard life was good. My friends and I talked about living difficult lives and enduring our hardships instead of simply making decisions which would make our lives easier.

During this time I had good self-esteem quite apart from my facade. I had a regular group of friends who treated me respectfully and were genuinely interested in being with me. During high school years, I would always have to call friends to hang out but my new group was proactive and reached out to me and this subtle gesture meant a lot. I thought my new facade was the reason for these friendships. I was unaware of my own best qualities, among which were affability and kindness. My life also felt meaningful with an increased work load and my conversations were more interesting. I could relate better to the people I lived with because most of my friends worked through college and my life was now similar to theirs.

The combination of alcohol and my highly-caffeinated nitrogen-based energy drink kept me happy because anyone going as little sleep as I was would have probably been miserable. One night during a party I ran so low on energy my heart began hurting so I went out and bought another energy drink to cure the pain. It somehow worked, but my body was running on sugar, vitamin b, and caffeine and was likely to break down at some point. The partying continued three or four nights a week, but the school work increased in difficulty and volume. My friends were now part of a fraternity and we hung out there regularly. They mentioned pledging now and then and thought it would be a good idea for me to join the frat so I could hang out with them whenever I wanted. Eventually I did.

Pledging was a difficult time, during which all my new-found freedoms from living on my own were taken away. Our pledge master was employed with the campus ROTC unit and had served overseas in the military. He made our pledging as militaristic as possible. The brothers constantly compared pledging to boot camp, as if we were being trained for our own well-being and survival. We met once a week for pledge "training" and were required to come to the house as often as possible to clean, work on projects, and just "hang out". During the week every brother in the fraternity would remind you of how awful your next meeting was really going to be, sometimes attributing this to the fact that you had done something wrong. Always, though, these threats were a means to feel superior and instill some fear in someone else. We pledges were required to clean the house an hour before every pledge meeting, while the pledge committee would sit in one of the nicest rooms of the house blasting death metal as a means of communicating they were preparing the worst for us. When the time for the meeting arrived, someone would send us into the pledge room where they'd make us wait. The idea was to create apprehension. Before entering the room, they'd wrap on the door with bats and metal chains and scream in anger about how awful the upcoming meeting would be.

During pledge meetings, we stood in a line as brothers stood face to face with us and yelled at the top of their lungs in our faces. Committee members were never allowed to hit anyone, but they brought baseball bats, metal chains, and sometimes a hatchet and would bang the weapons around as if they were going to use them. Sometimes they'd drive the weapons into the walls of the pledge room. One entire wall of this room, which was about twenty feet long, was missing all the dry wall and had only little scraps of plaster hanging from the studs; most of the pink insulation was visible.

In games designed to increase our drinking capacities, we were forced to drink exorbitantly which caused vomiting. We were punished, ostracized, and severely yelled at for mostly meaningless mistakes made during the week leading up to the meeting. Physical demands were made on us during the meetings, including special push-ups, wall sits, and other exercises intended as part of our "deserved" punishment. The pledge committee created an extreme fear of any wrong doing, to the point where making honest mistakes didn't seem to be all right. They wanted to convince us we deserved what we were getting.

In reality the brothers themselves were confused. No one deserves to endure pledging but none of us realized it at the time. The brothers said they believed the pledge process would create positive changes in our lives but I think most knew that no good would come of it. They were re-creating the same pledge experience they had endured and considered it a rite of passage. Most of the brothers did drugs and had many psychological issues but they never addressed their issues, so they took them out on other people. Besides intimidating the pledges, they would get into fights outside the fraternity on the weekend, when they were drunk and drugged.

The pledge committee was also responsible for the "moral training" of the pledges: ironically, they lectured us about great values such as honesty, respect, and integrity. Each of the brothers on the pledge committee represented a value. Although they taught values they weren't living up to, it was still useful to hear someone express them. During each meeting, there was a quiet time where we listened to lectures on values. I listened intently to the brothers when they spoke of ethical behavior, and people started liking me for it. The concept of integrity was increasingly important to me while pledging. I'd spent my freshman year in revelry and neglect; now for the first time in my life I was considered a man of integrity and people talked about how good a person I was.

This only contributed towards the mental rigidity that I would later experience with the development of schizoaffective disorder, when I became unable to navigate conversations where I disagreed with people. I felt great doing the right thing and my devotion to righteousness was beginning to pervade my life to the point where I wouldn't even joke about doing something wrong. My perception of there being a clear cut right and wrong instead of categorizing actions as relatively good or bad was problematic. Sometimes actions don't need to be perfect, they just need to be good or good enough, and this was something I didn't understand. I know I can strive to do my best now and if the consequences of my actions aren't perfect—but still create a good outcome—then that's perfectly acceptable. My thought that there was only one "right thing" was an indication that I expected perfection from myself. This perfectionism later became extremely problematic for me. I made it a point for people to know I was doing "the right thing" rather than just doing it.

The brothers created rules which had to be followed all over campus and they informed us that there were brothers everywhere and they'd be watching us. Some of the rules were house rules which required us to clean the house every week and complete projects such as building beirut tables and recycling beer cans. Other rules forbid us to enter through the front door and demanded that we run errands whenever asked. If ever one of us refused to do something a brother asked, there were severe consequences during that week's pledge meeting, like being made to drink until we threw up. At the time I was well-liked, so they didn't force me to do much, but some of the less popular pledges were constantly picked on and coerced into doing things. The frat wanted you to think it was the only authority you needed to answer to.

Although I wasn't working, pledging took up as much of my time and energy as a job would have, while my school work was increasing, and I was going out during the week and on weekends just as much as I had been the previous year. My mind was slipping and this led me to become fanatical in my adherence to good values. I was unaware of how to navigate social situations without compromising my beliefs; my conversations were becoming contentious. Even a sarcastic joke about unscrupulous behavior could set me off.

I was searching for meaning in absolutely everything and had lost my ability to have light-hearted, "meaningless" conversations. Many times people say things they don't mean—usually in good humor—but I took them literally and this created many arguments and awkward conversations. Light conversation is very helpful in creating mental flexibility and is a great stress reliever. I was so adamant about having a meaningful life, I came to think that if I didn't say exactly what I meant all the time, I would lose hold of my values and slip into my previous life of meaninglessness. I didn't understand it's mentally healthy to have and express a variety of different thoughts, some more "meaningful" than others. I thought even joking about bad behavior was wrong-doing in itself. I didn't understand the use of rhetorical devices such as sarcasm, which indicate that the behavior in question is ridiculous: laughing at ridiculous things means you understand they're things you wouldn't do.

During this time my mental clarity was decreasing. I thought that if I was as scrupulous as possible, it would improve or be restored. Hadn't focusing on good values always led to clarity of mind in the past? I became more rigid in my thinking, and I became afraid of the consequences for even the slightest and most honest of mistakes. Many people with schizoaffective disorder develop a rigidity in their thinking which becomes extremely problematic. This is when I started developing mine.

I thought it was my responsibility to inform everyone of how they should act when they were in the wrong. It was a fact that I had benefited from such correction myself. During pledging, someone had told me that I needed to "make the right decision" and from that point on I actually started making the right decisions again. As a result, I thought that it was my responsibility to tell every single person who was doing something wrong at that specific moment that they needed to change the way they were acting. Usually if people are going to change, they need to make that decision on their own.

Many times in conversation, when someone is in the wrong, no one tries to correct that person because it can be fairly awkward. The person who disagrees will usually make a neutral statement or subtly voice a disagreement and advance the conversation beyond the point of contention. This means the person in the wrong may never truly realize his error because out of politeness his listeners have given him reason to think he has their assent, which reinforces his wrong way of thinking. I thought I had to counter other people's delusional thoughts every single time that led to a lot of problems.

My rigidity in thought manifested itself in other ways too. I believed I had to be "a man of my word." I took this to the point where I believed that I had to do almost anything I had stated I would do, so I became extremely careful with my words. I also began believing in clichés, thinking that they've lasted for so many years because they are true—which is false. Many times, common misconceptions are carried throughout human history but aren't any more valid for having existed longer. Although *some* clichés are true circumstantially it was limiting for me to adopt these as universal truths to which I had adhere to in all situations. My adoption of clichés of righteousness contributed to the demise of my well-being. Living by a cliché is fairly limiting because you need to have the flexibility to change your mind and devise unique solutions to situations. I was searching for precepts which held true in all aspects of life but all you can do is make your best decision in a timely manner. All solutions are circumstantial.

"Carpe Diem" was one cliché I adhered to strongly. I felt I had to make the absolute most out of every single day. While this is a great thing to do, it neglects our necessity for rest and relaxation. Sometimes life is about relaxing and having fun, but I thought I had to constantly work. I began to hate television, preferring to do more important things. I didn't realize the importance of low-key activities and was always trying to do something which I deemed productive. This was a major factor in my increasing exhaustion.

I believed "if you don't have anything good to say

don't say anything at all," and constantly practiced this. People would say something they knew was morally wrong jokingly and I would return their humor with silence. This created ambivalence because I thought I was doing the right thing by not assenting to anything unscrupulous but deep down I knew it was rude and mean to stay silent after being spoken to. It was emotionally painful but I thought I was doing the right thing.

During the winter break I worked full time with a carpenter and I also kept a sales job. I was still strung out at this point and one morning, while driving to work, I rear-ended a pick-up truck. I was driving on the off-ramp going about 25 mph and it led into a rotary. I assumed the truck in front of me would keep going because there weren't any cars in the rotary. Continuing forward, I drove straight into the rear fender of the truck and was stopped abruptly. My engine was smoking and my car was towed, but the truck didn't have any damage and luckily no one was hurt. It really bothered me that this completely unexpected incident occurred. I was deeply upset and started realizing if I wasn't careful these sorts of things could happen. The incident stripped away my youthful illusion of invincibility. It made me extremely vigilant to the point where I decided I needed to start driving under the speed limit to prevent accidents. Although the accident definitely could have been avoided with better awareness, it wasn't a direct result of lacking vigilance and had nothing to do with speeding. Thinking the truck had gone ahead was a poor assumption, and was a direct result of mental exhaustion.

While working I became more cautious about the way I completed tasks, which hampered our productivity. My carpentry boss knew something was wrong but couldn't figure out exactly what. He told me I should feel on top of the world when in fact I felt completely beaten down by it and was trying to find my way. This attitude also affected my other winter job in sales, at which I did really well for one week, selling over $1000 in products. The sales manager was using sales techniques to motivate people to sell his products and I disagreed with his strategy. I knew that he was trying to create a positive work environment but I also knew his methods were monetarily incentivized. Businesses need to make money but it wasn't something I believed in at the time. I should have quietly resigned from the position but I made a scene over it, using an Abraham Lincoln quote which I had read in my pledge book as the basis for my argument. I told the sales manager how I thought what he was doing was completely wrong and how I was going to have nothing to do with it and stormed out of the room. He called me later that night. Aware that something was wrong in my life he suggested I get some help.

At this point I had been going for about eight months with about four to five hours of sleep on most nights, only occasionally getting a better night's rest, while placing high physical and mental demands on my body. I returned to school and spent at least another month pledging until we reached hell week. We were locked in the pledge room that entire week, only allowed to leave for food and classes. Showers were forbidden and the brothers ensured we had only one or two hours of sleep most nights; they demanded we drink exorbitantly every night of that week. The brothers kept one song repeatedly playing throughout the entire hell week to torment us. This is actually a technique used by military interrogators and I think our pledge master must have come up with the idea. They required us to wear diapers during all the meetings and they degraded us as much as possible. This was a time where I began pushing the limits of sanity and thinking some really odd thoughts. I became lightheaded and loopy but also learned that I could push my limits of wakefulness far further than I previously thought I could. It felt as if I were completing military training and it gave me a feeling of accomplishment because I felt I could endure something other people were possibly unable to.

They thought we had to endure this trial to become one of them, and they made the week as difficult as possible. At all the pledge meetings, high physical demands were made on us; I pushed myself so far past my limits during hell week that I actually passed out while doing push-ups. I was so drunk I didn't learn this until a later date when someone mentioned it in conversation. The entire pledging experience created a lot of anger in me, which I never consciously addressed. The brothers were convinced the pledge process was for the good of the pledges and would condition them to be better people. It definitely did the opposite. I started believing that all this anger and violence was for my own good in some way. That delusion was definitely reflected in my psyche. I started believing their means of discipline, such as yelling and instilling fear, were perfectly acceptable, when in fact such methods only create more problems without solving the original problems.

The experience created a skewed sense of friendship because the brothers believed punishing pledges was part of the process of becoming friends. In reality friendship is an entirely positive interaction and no one should have demanded anything from us or put us through any difficulties. Situations like this can only happen if you decide to allow them to happen to you. Allowing others to do awful things to me gave me the sense that I deserved them, which I did not. I just had difficulty standing up for myself because I had poor self-esteem. Most of my peers endured pledging because they wanted friends and an interesting college experience.

   After pledging I still kept a strict gym schedule, did my school work, went out three or four nights a week, and worked on improving the frat house through carpentry. I thought it had to be the best house it could be and started yelling at people who were unwilling to help me get it that way. The exterior was well-painted and the grounds were well kept but inside, it was a mess. There was always garbage littering the floors, tons of beer cans, and holes in the walls of every room. The floors were filthy and were stained a dark brown from all the dirt and soot that had been carried in. There were a lot of people who did things half-ass and I started getting on them instead of just letting it go. I believed in creating fear in others to coerce them into doing things because that had been so commonly practiced during my five months of pledging.

   I was edgy and was constantly sizing people up, speculating how well I would do in a fight against them. The fraternity created a sense of foreboding and I really began to feel as though the frat brothers were my only friends. It was "us against the world and all its miseries". Many of the brothers had short tempers and would start yelling in rages about how they would fight someone and what they would do to him. Others would flip out on their girlfriends and intimidate them into assenting to everything they were saying. I think some of their girlfriends only stayed with them because they were afraid of the consequences of breaking up. Some of the brothers would rip off their shirts and punch holes through the walls and then a few moments later they'd be laughing and joking. Although they tried to make it seem that their anger was meant in good humor, there was some earnestness in it. Most of the brothers were doing drugs that were far worse than marijuana and many had knives in their rooms. Some had 4"-5" hunting knives that they kept around but never actually used for hunting. They'd compare knives and marvel at the bigger and sharper knives, sometimes testing their efficacy on any object which they deemed trash such as walls, old furniture, and cardboard boxes. Many people kept baseball bats too and used them to destroy old furniture. There were other weapons in the house such as metal pipes, 2"x4"s, hatchets, and chains. Old furniture never lasted very long because someone always wanted to break something. The ROTC pledge leader had guns in his room and bought an AR-15; he tried to keep it a secret but failed miserably. The gun created a fervor in the house and everyone felt a renewed sense of confidence because they felt supported by the presence of this weapon. The presence of weapons possessed by such mercurial personalities was disconcerting. In the back of my mind I was uncertain whether one of these guys would snap one day.

The nitrogen-based energy drink which I had been using to power me through my days was losing its effect, and I was experiencing side effects, so I stopped taking it shortly after pledging. My energy level decreased.

I was also losing my connections with all my friends who were not fraternity members because I had been spending so much time at the house.

In the fall semester of my sophomore year I had failed an important class and was failing it again during the spring semester. I began to consider a different major. I thought about English as a major and knew it would be difficult, but I felt that I might diversify my career options by obtaining an English degree. At this point I had already taken many business classes so decided to make business my minor and switch my major to English starting my junior year. Most of my general education courses were also completed at this point. My hopes of passing the business classes I needed in order to progress within that major were minimal, so I made the switch and began English classes the fall semester of my junior year.

I retained tons of anger from my experiences in middle school, growing up, and pledging but was unwilling to admit or face any of it. People were making fun of me regularly again which was another thing I resented. I felt trapped and had no idea where to turn or how to change my predicament. I remembered that the brothers didn't always get along well with their parents, and I started thinking that all my problems were a direct result of the upbringing my parents gave me. I have great parents and this definitely wasn't the case but there were noticeable quirks in my personality which I traced directly to them. I started believing they were the reason I had endured the years of ridicule from middle school up to that point in my life. I intentionally avoided my family because I didn't want to hear any of their "delusional and meaningless words". This only contributed to my growing isolation. I believed they were supposed to be perfect people who I could model myself after. I only saw their imperfections; I considered everything wrong with me a direct result of modeling my behavior on theirs. I was angry they weren't perfect people; I still believed other parents were perfect and I blamed mine for being flawed. The majority of my own imperfections, for which I blamed them, were simply growing pains which naturally occur during most people's lives. I also thought my mental inhibitions were the reason for all the ridicule I had endured over the years. I blamed them for my having had a cognitive impairment, even though they never caused the mental deficiencies or the ridicule.

My life was beginning to reflect that of earlier

years where I felt meaningless and was picked on. During a relatively slow work week I experienced a storm of mixed emotions. I was alone in my dorm room one night, thinking about all the things in my life which weren't going the way I wanted, and about how I still felt disconnected from the people in my life. Simultaneously I felt good in some ways. My ambivalence turned to anger and I took my keys and cut three slashes into my forearms. It took a repeated effort but I was physically strong at the time and eventually created the cuts after repeated scrapings. They were deep but barely bled. I felt I had accomplished something by doing this.

While hanging out at a friend's dorm later that week, I was wearing a long sleeve shirt but rolled up the sleeves so everyone could see the scars. Someone jokingly said the cuts were really because I had poor self-esteem and cut myself, but I told my friends they were the result of manual labor at the fraternity. At the time, I had an idea I had psychological issues but still wasn't willing to broach any difficult subjects. Cutting my arms and rolling my sleeves wasn't a consciously thought out decision to ask for help, but I definitely felt I needed help at the time. In the back of my mind, doing this was some sort of effort to get attention which I hoped would lead to help. I didn't want to admit there was anything wrong in my life, but felt if someone else offered help it would be an acceptable way of getting what I needed. A member of the fraternity asked me one night if I wanted to talk about the cuts but I told him I'd be all right and didn't address any issues.

All the work I was doing created tons of stress and started sapping all the fun out of my personality; besides, I started believing people aren't allowed to have fun. I thought life was work, which for me at the time it was, because I made it that way. I believed I had to earn everything by my own merit; I was ashamed of coming from an affluent family because so many of my peers constantly ridiculed kids from affluent families as people who had been given a lot and had done nothing to deserve it. I thought my parents had spoiled me throughout my life. I saw that as the reason for my unhappiness. I wanted to prove I could earn my own living. I thought that, to fit in, I had to create the impression of being poor, because people around me were constantly talking about their lack of finances as though it was something to be proud of. I thought working extreme hours would convince others I was poor and it would allow me to lament with them.

The people I hung out with idolized the working-class hero. Nearly everyone claimed the rags-to-riches narrative for himself. I find this somewhat comical now because most of my friends were from out of state and they obviously had some form of help to pay for out of state tuition and if they really needed the money they would have went to an in-state school. Most of these kids were fairly affluent too.

That semester was the first time in my life when I actually felt a positive feeling in my heart, which soon, however, developed into mania. The sensation started in my heart and ran up through the left side of my throat. It was adrenaline being triggered from my thyroid gland, but at the time I had assigned a more spiritual meaning to it. I attributed it to my living righteously.

Before this actually happened, I thought people spoke of the heart metaphorically and it wasn't something palpable. The adrenaline I felt created an extreme lightness. Starting from my heart and passing up through the left side of my throat, the adrenaline felt electric and also felt as if a wispy flow of air had replaced the blood in my heart and veins. It spiked my energy levels without inducing the fogginess which adrenaline rushes usually cause. This feeling constantly flowed and increased in intensity while I inhaled and then slightly decreased in intensity while I exhaled. It felt like a drug-induced state and made me wonder why anyone would ever do any drugs if they could feel this way without drugs.

I think it was a physiological de-stressing mechanism because it only occurred once I started sleeping less and my stress levels increased. For several years after my second episode I felt the adrenaline when my medication wore off at night before bed and I have also felt it when I have missed doses of Risperidone. The Risperidone is an anti-psychotic that reduces my stress levels. I have felt the adrenaline less since taking beginning to take it, especially since adding .5 mg of Clonozapam to my prescriptions. I've felt this feeling since this time intermittently. I don't think it has anything to do with the nitrogen-based energy drink because I haven't taken that for years and I still get this exact feeling.

Before the semester ended we needed to decide if we'd be living in the house the next semester. The older brothers tried convincing new fraternity members to live in-house because having more tenants meant more money would be collected for the fraternity and the room rates would be reduced for everyone. They tried convincing everyone, regardless of how much or little they liked that person, just to get their money. I was still generally liked by most people in the fraternity so everyone encouraged me to live there.

One of my best friends who was outside of the fraternity wanted to live in an apartment for his senior year. After basically assenting to live together, I found out that another friend might be sharing the apartment with us, which would make our bedroom a triple. I had lived in a triple my freshman year and it felt crowded—I didn't realize that in an apartment the bedroom is only a sleeping space and we'd have the rest of the place to spread out and relax. I made an impulsive last second decision to live in the frat house and my friend was unable to get the apartment he wanted. This created a lot of tension between us and our friendship came to a standstill with very little conversation between us. Because we had the same group of friends and I didn't want to face him, my options for people to hang out with outside of the frat house during the upcoming year were limited.

At the time, I didn't believe in making apologies. I felt that apologies were meaningless and useless. After making a mistake I wouldn't say a word. Certain situations definitely require apologies (such as the ditching of a friend to live somewhere else) but I never actually gave one. Apologies are normal and acceptable and are a sign of respect, not of weakness.

Decisions like the one I made about my living arrangement started making me feel as though I was someone who didn't always make good decisions. It was definitely true that I'd made a bad decision by leaving my friend in the lurch at the last minute, but my image of myself as a bad decision maker only made me inclined to make more bad decisions.

The spring semester ended and I went back to the grounds crew I had worked for the previous summer, working mostly nights. Unfortunately, I picked up another landscaping job to work days. This meant that, between the two jobs, I'd be working 60 hours one week and 110 hours the next, alternately, all summer long. During work one day one of my coworkers started joking with me about the difficulty of the job. He was trying to tell me how much it sucked and I responded to his joke with complete silence. This silence made me feel awful, but at the time I didn't understand what to do because I thought if I had nothing good to say it wouldn't benefit me to say anything. I was also angry because my coworker was searching for reasons to be miserable, which was something I didn't want to do. Although I still don't enjoy complaining, I recognize now that I still needed to advance the conversation or change it in some positive direction, respectfully.

I was exhausted to the point where I always decided to say less words instead of more for lack of energy rather than economy of words. It got to the point where I stopped saying the word "No" or any words with any negativity in them because I thought refraining from uttering negative words would give me more energy and keep me positive. I could feel my facial muscles sagging from exhaustion and in the later hours of each day it was an effort to keep my eyes open. The bags under my eyes were extremely dark and drooped pretty low. People commented on them regularly. My muscles were always tight from manual labor and extra lifting at the gym. I blasted the air conditioner at night just to stay awake while driving home from work.

Before the summer ended I took a week off and traveled to a resort with my family, where I spent most of my time by myself. I spent most days in the hot tub sipping cool alcoholic drinks which my parents bought for me, and slept about fourteen hours a night in the hotel room. After a week of sleeping I felt partially restored to a regular energy level and my mind was functioning much better than before. But I still didn't realize that I needed to keep a regular sleep schedule. I felt compelled to push myself to my limits and thought I was proving something by doing so. In reality I only proved my ignorance of the human condition while diminishing my health. I bragged to my friends about the number of hours I worked every week and the difficulty of the labor. I thought I was making a great deal of money, because I was taking home more than I'd ever earned at any previous job. I was making $12.50/hr landscaping and $10/hr at my night job. Working 100 hours per week, this amounted to what seemed like a great paycheck. I didn't realize that if I put my effort into my school work and earned better grades, it would help me obtain a better paying job. The amount of money I'd make in the first year of my first job would far exceed that of any pay check I was likely to receive for the work I was doing. More importantly, I would have felt better physically and emotionally.

The fall semester of my junior year began with English classes, fraternity life, and a new landscaping job. At this point I was so unwilling to accept any help from my parents that I built my own bed frame out of 2"x4"s and left my mattress at home. Initially I was unable to buy a mattress so I put a futon pad over the boards. The padding of the futon slipped between the spaces of the boards comprising the bottom of the frame and I mostly felt boards sticking into my sides while attempting to sleep, but I still wouldn't ask them for anything. I was completely out of contact with my Dad and only spoke to my Mom periodically. We usually got into arguments because I misunderstood what she was saying. I was "ignorant and suspicious"(Joseph Conrad), vigilantly guarding against persuasion of any kind. I eventually bought my own mattress—two months later, when I found time.

I was able to obtain the rest of the furniture I needed from brothers who had moved out the previous semester and had left their old stuff in the house for anyone who wanted it. I left everything my parents had ever bought for me at home because it wasn't something I bought with my own money. I wanted not only to be able to tell people what I bought but what I was thinking while I bought it. I had perceived that people were resentful towards those who obtained things without working for them, and I wanted to be liked, so I ensured everything I owned was something I earned with my own money.

Regardless of the weather and season I always wore work boots, ragged light blue jeans, a white crew neck undershirt, and a light hooded sweatshirt.

I really enjoyed English classes because they had interesting conversations about life and the teachers genuinely cared for their students and subject matter. This resonated well with me so I started paying close attention to the lessons. Although the business teachers definitely cared for their students, the business lessons led me to believe otherwise, because the purpose of business is making a profit and the classes teach the logistics of doing so. At the time, English classes were the only positive influence in my life and I looked forward to each one. The English classes were only at the beginning level for the major but the amount of reading felt substantial. Up till then I had never been assigned reading of such volume. Although I was learning and improving, I struggled. But I obtained passing grades and found something I was passionate about.

The continual long days —the library, class, work, the gym, nights out, fraternity events, and work at the fraternity— took a toll on my mental health. I was still extremely irritable and yelled at people when I felt they weren't doing a good job. I still believed in all the clichés that I had accepted as truth, and I was difficult to get along with. I also had the unaddressed negative experiences of my past lingering in my subconscious, creating stress. My mind was muddled and was processing at much slower speeds than it previously had. Even with all the reading from class, conscious thought took immense effort. It took at least twice the amount of time and effort that it should have just to process simple thoughts. Even no-brainers were requiring some effort.

There had been times in the past when I was unable to pinpoint exact thoughts, but my mind was different at this point in my life. I could think consciously, and when I was well-rested—which was seldom—I could achieve some clarity. Exhaustion can immensely impede thinking. While I was exhausted, it took a great deal of effort to generate and sustain each thought.

Drawing the right conclusions and making the right decisions became far more difficult. I often settled for less effective solutions, partly because I was at a lower intellectual level, partly because I was young, but mostly because of exhaustion. My mind was becoming increasingly more muddled. Occasionally I made incoherent statements. I think with a well rested mind I would have never started believing in clichés and interpreting the world the way I was, but my mind worked very differently while I was worn out.

During work and at the fraternity I was always shoveling snow, which is exhausting work. I became pretty strong but I think the tightness that developed in my muscles also contributed towards my irritability and sleeplessness. I was always physically tense and this kept me alert and awake at night because it was difficult to find the comfort I needed to rest. I had difficulty sleeping because the house was poorly heated. Sometimes my roommate, who had a thick winter comforter, would open the window in the middle of the night because he was too hot and we argued back and forth as to whether it should be open or shut. I only had two throw blankets because of my unwillingness to accept anything I didn't buy with my own money. I was usually cold while attempting to sleep with the window open but he was persistent. He also had a mercurial mood—and he slept on the bottom bunk —so I didn't want to disturb him and climb out of bed all the time to keep warm.

Some days I actually did have time to sleep during the day but was so overtired I wasn't able to. My face was still sagging and people constantly commented on the bags under my eyes the way they had before. I started walking in as straight a line as possible because I thought if I could save some steps it would help save energy. I struggled to stay awake in class and missed portions of class discussions at times. I was interested in the material and really put forth a good effort to stay awake but still drifted off periodically. I was barely able to keep my eyes open because I was usually seated at a wooden desk in a heated room which was comforting in contrast to the conditions I was accustomed to.

I became tired of the fraternity and tired of its values and mostly started avoiding hanging out with everyone there altogether. I hated the pledge program and was resentful that anyone would ever want to put anyone else through any misery at all, never mind someone they supposedly cared about. I was resentful towards the brothers for their values and they reciprocated my feelings. I could see how negative these people were and disliked the way they treated others. I wanted to be different. I believed that the worst parts of my personality were a direct result of being with them. They were the reason for my loneliness! I made connections between my worst qualities and their personalities and never actually realized that I had decided to be the way I was. My problem was sleep deprivation and the onset of schizoaffective disorder, but I wasn't aware of that at the time. I developed a stoic disposition from sleep deprivation and loneliness but also from taking some cultural influences too close to heart.

Unfortunately, I was still living at the fraternity and drinking four nights a week. My alcohol tolerance and consumption had increased immensely. In past years, I was never someone who would black out from drinking because I felt the purpose of drinking was enjoying and remembering the night. I would usually nurse beers after I had a buzz, just to keep the buzz going. Once I was in the fraternity, I started drinking quantitatively, usually counting up to 20-25 beers per night and competing with others in alcohol consumption. Being a big drinker was a badge of honor; we associated manliness with the amount of alcohol we drank. This led to a lot of arguments and to blackouts. These occurrences contributed to the mounting tension and distance which existed between myself and the brothers.

I was eventually the least liked person in the house because of my contentious behavior and there were two occasions where people picked fights with me. I felt completely isolated from everyone and avoided most conversations. During those four months, I wasn't hanging out anywhere other than at the house, because I didn't know anyone outside of it any more. People would usually come over to party and hang out so there were people to be with who weren't fraternity brothers. I would stay in because it was easier than going out. Besides, I wasn't invited anywhere. I was no longer friends with anyone in the fraternity and wasn't in contact with my old friends who weren't a part of it. People would constantly bang on my door in the middle of the night while I was trying to sleep just to wake me. There was an unspoken resentment between myself and most of the brothers. Although we sat together during meals and fraternity events, my friendships were fractured. Hostility set in.

This is when a new feeling—which at the time I labeled "affliction"— began to affect me. I now believe they were anxiety attacks There was initially a sharp pain in my heart that would subside but still persist. It felt as if someone had my heart in a vice press from all sides and there was no way to get out of it. It felt like my heart was being restricted and constantly hurt. For some reason, the only way to really get rid of this feeling was by working hard. I mostly felt affliction after being terse with someone, not laughing at a joke, or after ignoring someone, and many times after making even the slightest of mistakes. There had been some impulsive decisions I'd made while drinking that I worried about because they contributed to the growing distance between myself and the fraternity brothers. It's important to note that the mistakes I made while drinking were impulsive but minor and were nothing I could have gotten into any trouble for. But I had come to believe that if I made even the slightest of mistakes it would increase my isolation. Every time I made even the simplest and most honest of mistakes I felt affliction from anxiety.

I believed in karma; I thought I must have done something awful to deserve the awful quality of life I had at the time. It struck me that these mistakes must have been the reason for my misfortune, even though I was a good person. I didn't understand that sometimes bad things just happen to good people and this was one of those cases. Unfortunately, I was mentally exhausted and unable to understand that many things in my life were contributing to the diminishment of my health. I also failed to consider that the quality of my life had already immensely diminished well before any of these impulsive decisions were made. I think another component of my belief that I must have done something wrong was my having been frequently told I was in the wrong during my childhood. People constantly pointed out my mistakes when I was growing up, scapegoated me, and ridiculed me for things that I had nothing to do with; I had fallen into habit of thinking I was always at fault. I had poor self-esteem and it seemed natural for me to blame myself for anything that went wrong regardless of the situation. This created issues for me because I feared loneliness more than anything. My fear of loneliness only increased my mental rigidity; I felt I had to control everything about myself to ensure I didn't make any more impulsive decisions that would create more distance between myself and others. My belief that I had done something wrong-was strong enough to contribute to my mental rigidity and affect my health. The desire to control every facet of my life was omnipresent throughout both my episodes. I was afraid of making mistakes for a number of reasons, partly because I had made some mistakes which created loneliness for me.

In later years I learned that, even though the development of schizoaffective disorder was not my fault, I still had to to gather, create, and develop resources that I could use to make my life the way I wanted it to be.

There were many times when I was terse with people in conversation and this made people angry at me. I was unable to joke sarcastically while adhering to the cliché, "if there's nothing good to say don't say anything at all". People are accustomed to lengthier conversations in which the other person listens and responds to their thoughts. When I only provided very short responses, people would interpret those responses as me simply not wanting to talk to them. People would usually address me kindly, expecting kindness in return, but after not receiving it they would be somewhat angry. Who could blame them? I misinterpreted their anger during these situations as a general dislike for me. This was isolating, and created the affliction feeling.

I also still felt the manic feeling after working diligently —I always felt good whenever I was working hard—but when I didn't complete tasks perfectly I felt affliction. My emotions strongly motivated me to become a perfectionist because one extreme felt nearly euphoric while the other was very painful; I felt awful after making even the slightest of mistakes.

Emotions were very influential in my decision making. I felt compelled to eliminate negative emotions and I was also compelled to perpetuate and or augment positive emotions. Emotions are usually changeable because they are derivatives of pieces of consciousness. In later years, I have developed an ability to pinpoint the thought within my psyche creating a negative emotion and I've been able to say or write the correct medicinal words to diffuse the emotion. This is something most people do regularly by talking about issues in their lives.

During schizoaffective disorder I experienced extreme emotions such as the affliction feeling which I dreaded and the maniacal feeling which I became addicted to. One difficult part of having bipolar disorder with schizophrenia is that the schizophrenia component disabled my reasoning ability, which made it more difficult to find the pieces of consciousness creating the emotions being experienced. Sometimes these emotions were simply physiological effects of being overexhausted. There was also the maniacal feeling triggered by stress relief. Being unable to rationally think about the emotions I was experiencing led me to conclude that my emotional extremes resulted directly from my "righteousness," or lack thereof. Deciding my emotions were directly related to my "righteousness," I strove to act as righteously as I possibly could, which resulted in extreme dis-functionality.

Having determined that righteousness was the reason for my adrenaline feeling, thus associating righteousness and mania, caused more maniacal feelings to occur any time I was doing something I deemed righteous. Subconsciously I thought if I did everything as well as I could—if I became a messiah!—I would re-unite with my family and make amends with lost friends and my problems would be solved.

It got to a point where I thought everything was a moral decision and had to be done as well as possible. I expected to feel an adrenaline rush if things were done correctly, which I liked at the time, but also feared feeling afflicted if mistakes were made.

I developed a rigid self-perception and envisioned myself as a morally righteous worker, who would make his way through life's difficulties with an unbreakable stoicism. I thought I was someone who wasn't to be messed with and was as tough as nails but who was nice to people if they were doing the right thing. I thought people would like me for being this way and did my best to stick to it. I think it's important to note my self-perception, because I believe others with mental illnesses develop personalities and ways of being for the same reason I did; they are convinced that it will make people like them. I became obstinate in my ways because I believed my new personality would yield good results. This rigidity in personality created a lot of awkward social situations. I was restricting thoughts and emotions to those I believed would fit the character type I had created for myself. Positive social interactions require a good amount of mental flexibility which was something I did not allow myself at the time.

I also didn't allow people to make fun of me much. Allowing others to joke with me became extremely problematic. When I was younger I was made fun of a lot for my lack of intelligence and I hated being made fun of. Now I was trying to create a personality that no one could make fun of.

Throughout my adolescence, I was partially cognitively impaired with thought blocking and racing thoughts and was still that way during my college years. I felt I was always in the wrong because people constantly ridiculed me, found fault in my actions, and made me a scapegoat. I couldn't figure out why I was forced to endure all the ridicule. Now I felt the same ridicule and fault finding that had occurred during my adolescence directed toward me again. I thought I must have been a terrible person for all of this to occur and strove to be as good as possible; I needed to become as scrupulous as possible to eliminate all the ridicule. I had become an odd person from exhaustion, overwork and isolation. I was different than most people but I meant well and I usually made good decisions.

People often commented on how hard I worked, so I developed a positive association with the way I worked. It was the one reason anyone in the frat house ever complimented me or spoke at length with me. I felt I might be more popular if I could continue creating good results through hard work.

Deep down I had a fear of being lonely which I had developed in middle school and had never addressed. I would do anything to ensure I was part of the group.

I came to believe the only way to eliminate everyone's resentment was to keep perfecting everything I was doing. I didn't realize that my contentious behavior —my attempt to be "righteous"—was the main reason for the chasm between myself and the frat brothers. Someone felt the need to tell me there is a point where something is good enough and then you should move on. I never listened to him, believing that everything could always be improved upon.

I think there's a difference between improvement and obsession; at that time, I was obsessive. My perfectionism was prevalent in every aspect of life. I refolded t-shirts multiple times ensuring all the lines on the shirts matched perfectly. I cleaned to the point where there were no visible specks of dust. I took extra time placing objects down, ensuring they were positioned as properly as possible. I started washing my hands as perfectly as I possibly could. I ensured I had a good lather which covered every visible spot on them and then rinsed to the point where they started chaffing; eventually my hands were completely cut up and bloodied. I washed them as frequently as possible. There were so many cuts it looked as though I had buried the backs of my hands in a bucket of small glass chips and moved them back and forth for a while. They were completely dried out, and I had three rows of substantial calluses on my palms. People noticed. They'd ask what had happened to my hands and I would say I fell on the ice. But most people knew something was wrong.

Part of my over diligence resulted from my inability to relax. There was so much resentment between myself and the fraternity brothers that I was constantly on edge, wondering whether someone would want to pick a fight with me. I already felt awful from the resentment the brothers expressed in their actions and words towards me; I think it deeply affected me because it reminded me of my middle school experience. People would ignore me and didn't want anything to do with me. I was constantly expecting the worst. I started developing a paranoia that anything could happen at any time. I began to be extremely careful at all times.

After a blackout in February I decided that I needed to stop drinking. I thought drinking was definitely the cause of all my problems so I quit cold turkey. Almost immediately afterwards I noticed some changes in my thinking and in my processing speed. My stream of consciousness was much clearer and I felt refreshed.

I was actually sleeping a little more but was still fairly busy with all the activities I was still involved in. I regained my sense of smell which had been missing for the past couple years. My visual clarity improved and life became more detailed. I was able to see farther and better and colors became noticeably brighter. I started losing some weight but at this point I was still 5'9" and weighed about 195 lbs and was in excellent physical condition. I still hung out in the fraternity on weekend nights and usually filled an empty beer can with water and refilled it a few times to avoid people peer-pressuring me to drink.

I started reconnecting with friends from freshman year and getting out of the house, which was excellent for my well-being. My energy levels were actually increasing because of the absence of alcohol in my system.

The reading requirements for school increased. I was spending more time at the library. I really started immersing myself in my studies and read about eight hours a day. During an average week, I would go to the library six days, usually from 2:00 pm until 2:00 am when it closed. I was still pushing the limits of my consciousness and considered it a badge of honor to stay awake for as long as I could. My mind was exhausted. Although I kept looking at the words on the page, I wasn't consciously processing or remembering much of anything. I was well aware of this, but I still put forth the effort to learn. Even having read the book, I needed to pay attention in class to get the plot outline and gain a general understanding of the literature. I used what I learned in class to write my papers. I didn't take class notes because I wanted to fully concentrate on memorizing the professor's words rather than divide my attention between listening and writing. I also knew I didn't have time to reread class notes later due to the busyness of my schedule.

We read mostly fiction in English classes. I came to believe there were portents in life, and if I interpreted them correctly, it would help me determine whether I was on a good path, doing the right thing. In town, the street lights were on timers which periodically turn off and on. At any given time of night, some of the lights are off while most are left on. This keeps the paths well lit while saving electricity and increasing the longevity of the bulbs. I watched lights at random searching for signs of whether I was on a positive path; if one of the few which happened to be off turned on, I interpreted it as a good sign and felt good about what I was doing. If one that was on turned off, I became apprehensive and self-conscious. I began thinking about what I had been doing and what my plans were at that moment—What could potentially cause something bad to happen?

While in the car I listened for particular songs on the radio which would indicate how I was doing in life and if I was in the right place. Because many songs playing on the radio are about feelings that almost everyone has experienced, it was easy to find parallels between the music and my life. I was searching for meaning and understanding. Occasionally I'd hear lyrics like these: "And I still haven't found / What I'm looking for." I would actually believe that—during that particular moment in time—I wasn't where I wanted to be in life. Coincidentally enough I wasn't happy with my life during this entire stretch, so it seemed as though this song and others were speaking directly to me. I listened intently for signs on the radio, not realizing that many stations have play lists of about twenty songs, and if I continued listening to the same stations I would hear the same exact songs conveying the same "signs" over and over again; my thinking would be cycling with the radio's play lists. I eventually figured out that the

52

songs were in a cycle but thought I would just need to look elsewhere for portents and indicators instead of dispelling the idea of portents completely.

I really listened intently to my professors, but I felt conflicted about values. There were many bad values I was trying to replace from earlier years with positive values I had learned from literature. I thought my values were the reason for my atrophy—and they did in fact cause some of my problems. Unfortunately, I didn't realize I was a good person who was experiencing a difficult illness. Many of my problems were from cognitive impairment and emotional impairment developing into schizoaffective disorder.

In the fraternity people were constantly talking about who they hated, who they planned to beat up next weekend, who they beat up last weekend. I knew there were people there who didn't like me. For my part, I despised most of the brothers. I directly connected their values to my problems. Many people at that age do the right thing but think it's cool to talk about doing the wrong thing. For me, thoughts directly influenced actions; I worked for uniformity in my thoughts and actions. I felt if I assented to any fallacious thoughts I would start to believe them, which would be detrimental towards my well-being. Many times I responded to sarcastic remarks with complete silence. This created contentious relationships and deterred people from talking to me. Many people were so accustomed to everyone readily agreeing to whatever it was they were saying, they didn't know what to do when I completely disagreed with them, without saying a word to explain my point of view. They misinterpreted my silence and thought I declined to respond out of malice. Though I disliked most of them at the time, I never intended anyone any harm.

I thought I needed to change as a person but

didn't know how to change; I didn't have a well-defined idea of who I wanted to be. I didn't realize most of my trouble was from sleep deprivation and the development of schizoaffective disorder. I lost trust in everything I knew.

I feel that experience may be common to most people with schizoaffective disorder. The loss of control that I felt stemmed from my inability to consciously define my thoughts and think my way through situations. I gathered bits and pieces of information but couldn't process them the way my mind can now. My attention would sway from one thought to another and I was unable to articulate all the ideas I wanted to express. Life was moving so quickly it felt as though I had little to no control. The illness is completely disorienting—everything seemed to happen at an accelerated pace.

I thought if I made neutral, ambiguous statements, it would enable me to more easily refute and dispel them if I later learned better. I did this only when speaking about abstract ideas, because I still believed that facts should be presented as facts: for example, this ink is black, this paper is white. My speech and my English papers reflected my unwillingness to completely assent to any idea. I included extra phrases before each statement in my speech and in my essays to express uncertainty, such as "I think", "I believe", "it seems as though", and " it feels as though" even when the statements were simply the truth.

This was fueled by the belief that I could always improve, which is definitely true, but I was unaware that I could replace old ideas with better ones as I learned them, even if the old ones had been stated as a certainty.

I wanted to create as much freedom and independence in my thinking as possible. Often, in conversation, I had experienced a loss of control, especially while pledging the fraternity. The feeling of lacking control also stemmed from schizoaffective disorder because I was unable to hold information in my mind and express my ideas with clarity. I had racing thoughts and had difficulty maintaining and creating clear ideas within a clear and comprehensible internal monologue. Bits and pieces of thoughts entered and exited my mind rapidly, eluding my ability to control them. This resulted in me copying the thoughts and ideas of those around me rather than thinking for myself, because I had a lot of difficulty thinking with any clarity.

During conversations, many people will make statements which are intended to elicit particular responses. I was unaware that I didn't have to respond in the way they expected and could respond however I preferred so long as I was respectful. There were many times when I was silent after someone made an emotionally persuasive statement.

I also wanted to present information objectively and allow others to determine their own opinions; I felt that if I clearly labeled my thoughts as nothing more than my personal opinions, I wouldn't be telling other people what to think; I'd be leaving them free to decide what to believe for themselves. I thought this would be reciprocated and would create mental freedom for both of us. I expected others to be as objective and impartial as I tried to be. When this didn't occur, I was disappointed.

I felt that at some point I must have been corrupted; I blamed other people for making me believe the things I came to believe. This feeling motivated me to never be persuaded into doing anything I didn't want to do ever again. It also motivated me to work hard to liberate my mind as much as possible. I wanted to live genuinely and think independently. When I heard people speak with emotion I felt they were trying to sway my opinion, to get me to agree with them. Often when I felt manipulated that way I would respond with complete silence. I didn't understand that I am free to think whatever I want regardless of how persuasive someone is trying to be.

At first my over-diligence was a strategy to fit in but eventually became obsessive. I believed I needed to work as hard as possible at all times to earn my way in life. I was searching for meaning. I even stopped eating breakfast, for this reason: Having been given the gift of life, I felt that I had to give something in return each day before eating the food which would make possible the continuation of my life. I thought everyone should obtain everything completely by their own merit.

While in the fraternity everyone was always asking for a favor, whether it be buying them alcohol, covering a sober duty, or loaning them something I owned —and they usually attempted to make me feel I owed it to them. I felt used. It got to a point where I was actually counting favors, trying to make the tally absolutely even with everyone so no one would ever have to ask me for anything again. I became concerned with being as even with everyone as I possibly could in all respects. I was unaware that it's easier to simply do what's best and respond to needs as they arise rather than creating a merit and compensation system.

There was one time when I woke up at 7am, worked from 8am-12pm, went to class, went to the library to complete my reading until 2 am the next morning, then wrote a paper at the frat house, then stayed up the rest of the night completing a project which I presented that morning at 8 am, then went back to work after class and got back to my room in the fraternity the next day at about 1 pm. I was constantly pushing my limits and going on increasingly less sleep.

People were becoming noticeably kinder towards me and the resentment was tapering off, but I still hated the fraternity for the pledge program and the way I had been treated in the past. In some ways, I was learning how to interact more congenially but in many others, I was still quite contentious.

Although many of my relationships had improved, some were still fractured. One night someone threw a beer bottle through my window claiming it had been an accident. After speaking to the person, it was obvious to me that the act had been intentional. This was disconcerting and created apprehension. About a week later there was another occurrence. My roommate, who was also less popular in the fraternity, was in the basement on a Saturday night and someone held a broken beer bottle pointed towards his throat and threatened to kill him in earnest. He told me about it later but I didn't want to take either side for fear of becoming entangled in the situation. He was a really strong guy—about 5'6", 225 lbs—and he challenged the guy who threatened him to a fight and hospitalized him. The fight was quick and brutal. The guy who threatened his life was about 6'2", 175 lbs, and was well liked. Everyone was cheering for him. He took one shot to the stomach, fell to the floor, then was punched in the face multiple times. His head shot back so hard it bounced a few inches off the wooden floor. Everyone rushed to pull my roommate off him as he threw a couple more punches before he was restrained. After the fight, everyone felt quite eery. This only increased everyone's dislike of my roommate. Most people didn't know the tall guy had threatened his life earlier that night and neither person was willing to tell anyone.

Finals came and I passed my classes and I figured out which classes I needed to complete to graduate on time. Switching majors at sophomore year's end required me to take summer courses to graduate on time, so I signed up for one summer class and kept my job with the company I had worked with throughout the school year. This enabled me to live at the fraternity and go to class. My work weeks were 40 hours but my manager accommodated my school schedule, which allowed me to take morning classes and work later into the day. After working days, I studied and read in a common room in the fraternity.

Chapter 2
Schizoaffective in Full Effect

One day I started thinking about how I got to be a friendless person who was completely alienated from everyone in his life. I examined the reasons for this and determined that before I was in the fraternity, life was pretty good, but since then it had been fairly miserable. I attributed the deterioration of my quality of life to having joined the fraternity and having assented to the poor values the brothers instilled through their ridiculous behavior. I hadn't factored in my sleeplessness and wasn't willing to admit I had any cognitive impairments, even though I knew I'd had cognition problems my entire life. I wasn't aware of the many unresolved issues I had from experiences while younger. I also didn't acknowledge the fact that I decided to join the fraternity and subjected myself to this environment.

I only knew this was a terrible place and didn't want to be affiliated with people who were responsible for corrupting and psychologically damaging so many others every semester, so I decided I needed to immediately cut off all ties with the fraternity. The house was fairly empty during summers and the people who were living there with me that summer were away, but I was afraid if I didn't leave that very moment I would never be able to.

I was somewhat of a conformist still and sometimes allowed others to influence my decisions. Knowing that about myself made me afraid I might remain a member of this place forever. It would riddle my life with its negative influence if I stayed any longer. This was the first time in my life I was seceding from a group in a social situation and it was an important decision for me. I was still in the habit of just going with the flow. I had to fight off small racing thoughts telling me me to stay with the group. I was fearful I might actually change my mind and decide to stay, so I started packing my stuff as quickly as possible. I used garbage bags to pack most of my clothes and I fit all of my belongings into my sedan. I tied my mattress to the top and left the rest of the furniture for whoever wanted it because it was all borrowed. There were shelves in the walls but I thought it would take too much time to dismantle them so I left them for the next person who would be living in that room and I took off for home as quickly as possible. (At this point in my life I always drove under the speed limit believing that if I went even the slightest bit over it I could cause an accident.)

I arrived home 55 minutes later and carried my stuff in, refusing the help of my family. I didn't want to talk to my family and I was completely out of contact with the people I had grown up with. I had stopped emailing, calling, and returning most calls sent my way. Some high school friends had tried contacting me but I'd ignored the ones I remembered as being the most disrespectful. For those that were respectful I usually informed them I was busy working and didn't have time to hang out.

I even carried my mattress to my room and slept on it during my stay, even though my room already had a bed set up. I went downstairs for meals but otherwise spent most of my time at home in my room. I talked with my mom infrequently and didn't say much to my dad. I was still attending classes and working and was up until 2 am every night reading. In the morning, I drove 55 minutes to school for morning classes which started at 7 am and woke up at 5:30 to arrive on time. I was still pretty exhausted but the adrenaline from ma-nia was becoming stronger and I began growing even more restless. Even when I was tired I usually forced myself to stay awake to complete homework.

I was afraid to say or do anything that anyone else wanted me to. This was from thinking the fraternity brothers' values had caused me to fall into a bad state of being. I was apprehensive about any bad influences sneaking their way into my life and creating other problems or exacerbating the current loneliness I was experiencing. I didn't want to feel persuaded into doing anything because I had previously been persuaded to join the fraternity and that was the worst time of my life up to this point.

I also blamed my parents for my disposition and attributed my worst qualities to having modeled my behavior on theirs. I wanted to blame anyone other than myself for my problems and never realized the problems weren't anyone's fault in particular.

I didn't want to say anything in class because at this point I was petrified of doing anything wrong because of the affliction I had connected to imperfection. One of my professors knew I was intentionally quiet and he thought it was because I hadn't read so he started questioning me on some of the literature we were studying. He merely wanted everyone in class to participate, but I took it as an effort to force me to talk. Of course, he *was* in fact trying to get me to talk, but I misinterpreted his intentions. We were reading short stories at the time and he asked me about a story about a fletcher and I informed him I was more interested in the baker. He knew about the baker's story and asked me questions about him but I returned his questions with some murmurs and he moved on to a different student.

I was driving to school from home that summer and arrived late for class one day. When I was late for a second class my professor pulled me aside and formally kicked me out of his class. This experience only made me feel as though I had done something else wrong when I was really putting forth my best effort; I was just exhausted.

I wanted to move back out of my parents' house and eventually found an apartment in the town where my school was located. Using money I had saved from working, I moved there. It had one door which opened into the kitchen, a small open closet to the right, a full bathroom further to the right, and the bedroom which was 5'x10' on the left. By myself, I moved everything I owned into that apartment, declining the help my family had offered. That summer I spent most of my time in isolation and continued demanding perfection of myself in every aspect of life. For the most part I completely secluded myself from my family, due to resentment, because I still believed they were responsible for instilling poor values in me during my childhood and were the reason for most of the anguish I had experienced (which definitely wasn't true).

The extent of my possessions was very limited. I left my mattress at home and was sleeping on a tile floor without a pillow. Since I had never bought any furniture with my own money, I never brought any from home. I spent most of my time either standing, sitting, or laying on the floor. Discomfort kept me wide awake many nights until I would drift off for three or so hours out of sheer exhaustion.

At work I was usually assigned cemetery maintenance which was very peaceful. The work was cutting and trimming the grass, but I thought to "honor the dead" I had to make every part of the cemetery as perfect as possible and spent entire days on plots that were merely 40'x40,' which was ridiculous. I paid no attention to how long it took me to do a job, believing that if everything was done perfectly the first time, no one would need to return to it. In the long run there'd be less work to do. It didn't occur to me that grass just keeps on growing. There is a time when a job is done well enough and we have to move on in order to complete the other work that needs to be done. When I should have been moving on, I stayed to perfect literally every single blade of grass I could see.

This was occurring was because my mania was perpetuated and increased whenever I felt I was doing something to the best of my ability. Having mania is like having a drug addiction because there are stimuli which create the euphoria of it, the same way alcohol or drugs induce effects, and it becomes difficult to deny yourself the feeling. Mania feels far better than any amount of alcohol I've ever had, probably better than any drug could feel. Mania creates positive emotional effects but with an alertness and clarity which alcohol and drugs lack. The mental clarity in particular was addicting for me, especially since I'd had so much difficulty finding mental clarity throughout the entirety of my life up to this point. The stimuli for me was *scrupulousness* — which probably holds true for many people with mania. I did everything I could to feel mania and it kept me wide awake and was a major contributor to my loss of sanity. Although I now had a clearer internal monologue, I was still thinking extremely irrational thoughts.

I was addicted to this natural feeling, which I thought was created through scrupulousness and diligence, and was completely unwilling to relinquish it because I had never felt this way in my life. (It does actually feel ecstatic.) It got to the point where my boss commented on how he thought I needed to speed up my work pace—"This isn't Disney Land"— but I persisted. He later spoke to me about drug addiction trying to determine whether I was using anything. He suggested I get some help.

Although I was out in the world working, we were

given individual assignments to cut and trim particular places in town which were usually void of people, and I really started living too much inside myself. My conversations were only with myself and I went days without saying more than several words to a few people. I began laughing aloud at my own jokes (which still happens today occasionally), which created many awkward moments. I did this whether I was with people or alone. This was partially because I had no one else to laugh with and felt compelled to laugh. I thought I should be able to laugh whenever I wanted, but this was quite startling to people whose social custom is to only laugh from external stimuli while with others.

A difficult facet of having schizoaffective disorder at this age for me was my yearning for independence. I'd always been told what I had to do or should do and now I wanted to be entirely independent. I began eliminating as many social norms as I possibly could simply because they felt confining. I hated the idea of having any type of rule for any situation. This is where I began getting out of touch with social customs. Although such behavior in schizophrenia patients is diagnosed as a symptom, I think in my case it was mostly caused from having experienced so much regulation and scrutiny from multiple sources throughout the course of my earlier years.

I eventually developed a complete aversion to anything even remotely related to convention. I sought ways to eliminate any and all rules in my life and it got to the point where I wouldn't use the word "normal". I substituted "regular" for "normal" and didn't start using the word normal again until four years after my second episode. I believed normal meant average; for me it had the connotation of convention and restriction, so I avoided doing anything I thought was normal. It's important to note that although normal means average it also means free of neurosis and psychosis. When I decided to avoid normality, I was making a decision to do strange things— to do anything that I thought differed from conventionality. I believe many of the eccentric behaviors I practiced during schizoaffective disorder episodes developed from my attempt to avert the control I felt conventionality had imposed upon me.

Growing up with a cognitive impairment had also felt very restricting and limiting mentally. This inhibition created a desire to liberate my mind in any and all ways possible. Though some of what I did was the result of sleeplessness, other behaviors had philosophical underpinnings. Only later did I realize that it's good to be normal in many instances and that being normal won't restrict me from achieving any goals I'm pursuing. In many cases it will help; even if those goals require achievements that are far beyond average.

Knowing we are constantly constructing our own realities and they do not exist intrinsically has been an important fact in my understanding of mental illness. We develop habits and beliefs that we repeat given the way we have constructed meaning from experience, and these repetitions contribute to the improvement or decay of our health. My desire to step out of the patterns of a life I didn't enjoy in my younger years led me to change my thinking patterns and my behaviors to more irrational ones to avoid repeating past experiences, such as being heavily derided in school and feeling so passive that I had absolutely no agency whatsoever. I was trying to step out of the bounds of my patterns of behavior and create a different way of life. But in doing so, I also left behind my healthier and more rational behaviors.

As I digressed I wasn't certain which behaviors had previously been working for me and which ones were problematic. I decided I needed to change absolutely everything about myself. Lacking control over my life left me feeling very helpless. I thought creating rules and regulations and precepts for every situation would give me more control—but this only developed mental rigidity which restricted and inhibited my thinking. At this time I had two completely contradictory ideals I was striving for, which caused a lot of problems. On the one hand, I wanted to feel freedom from having been so mentally inhibited, so I broke down almost every previous rule that I had followed till then, in order to feel liberated from my restrictions of earlier years. Contrarily, having been ridiculed as unintelligent, after I broke down an old rule I made an effort to replace it with a new rule in an effort to become more intelligent. The issue with my new rules was I didn't allow myself the mental flexibility to break them when necessary; I treated them as ultimate and universal truths that I had to adhere to with no exceptions.

As a result, I started creating rules for conduct and searching for precepts and universal truths which I would apply to every situation in my life. I didn't realize that any rule is usually only applicable in a certain situation, that to function at an optimal level I needed a balance between mental flexibility and control. Any meaning anything has is relational; identifying the relations between things and being able to adjust accordingly is a matter of mental flexibility. Our lives generally consist of our relationships to things outside ourselves, and sometimes between different parts of our minds. A mentally flexible mind is able to adapt and adjust to whatever circumstances it encounters. Having mental flexibility and agility has proven to be the easiest and most highly functioning way for me to think.

My adoption of rules and universal truths gradually gradually led to the onset of my episodes. I lost focus in steps and stages as I created each rule and "truth," increasingly distancing me from my healthier ways of life. My health decayed over time because I spent so much time in isolation. Being isolated made it difficult for me to figure out what was socially acceptable and how to functionally interact within society because I had very little interaction with other people. I was creating rules and restrictions that contradicted past behaviors, cultural norms, normality itself, and any number of things which I believed contributed to the unhappiness of my younger life, which I deemed unbearable. I looked for ways to become smarter, to have more control over my life, and to become more likable. Over time, I completely lost sight of my previous life, which had been far healthier than what my life had now become.

My digression happened the way a car drives down a road away from a comfortable place and eventually passes over the horizon. The driver can not see the road he left behind and doesn't know how to get back there or have any desire to. In this case, passing over the horizon into a new place was not a positive thing and I wasn't in a good place. To be sure, I passed over multiple horizons, and it took time to get back to a place where I was able to determine what is healthy and what is unhealthy. As I recovered after my episodes I was able to look back, to determine where I had been and compare that to where I was.

Part of recovery finding a new destination that is a way of life you find acceptable which is also healthy. The problem I initially confronted in my own recovery was returning to my old ways of being and finding myself unhappy again. I was searching for a new way of life. The key was creating a new way of life that was different from my earlier years, acceptable, enjoyable, and also healthy.

If I'd had help identifying which past behaviors

worked and which didn't, it would have improved my mental health. I also think developing agency through reading and participating in a healthy combination of active and passive activities also would have helped me.

As I lived in complete isolation, my delusional thoughts only continued at night; I started spending a great deal of time in reverie. I ruminated over every single moment of my life and began obsessing over my conscious thoughts to the point where I wouldn't allow myself to process "no-brainers" — I had to think everything through from beginning to end. I wanted to be the conscious agent creating every occurrence in my life. I recognized my younger self as somewhat impulsive and thoughtless. Now I had found a way of thinking things through and I wanted to do everything possible to hold on to it, because I believed it could fade away just as easily as it had been developed.

This time in my life was a mental awakening. I was beginning to live in the moment and consciously make decisions which I knew would impact my life. I didn't realize this mental clarity had been created from the mental exercise of school work, instead attributing it to my perfectionism. I thought if I regressed in my standards in any way I would completely lose the clarity.

The adrenaline type feeling was also becoming stronger and I felt it for the greater part of every day while working to the best of my ability. I considered it a moral breach to leave a job unfinished, but my evaluation of completion was extremely skewed and perfectionistic.

At this point it is safe to say I had lost all traces of sanity. For me losing sanity was meant a complete disconnection from all the habits and precepts that had kept me mentally healthy. One of the primary reasons this happened was mental exhaustion. When the mind is tired, conscious processing becomes far more difficult than it is while well-rested. It also becomes more difficult to filter ridiculous thoughts. If you are spending a great deal of time in isolation while mentally exhausted, you can begin allowing your mind to believe in concepts which are completely ridiculous. I began to adhere to delusions that I had created, which was debilitating. I had developed many delusions as a result of having an unclear stream of consciousness for years, and these thoughts were all working against me. One of the main reasons I had developed these delusions was my inability to process language and express my thoughts clearly. I was settling for less intelligent answers simply because I lacked the energy to think at length until I found the best answer.

I had been going for nearly two years with minimal rest and I was in a different realm mentally. My mind felt completely weightless and everything I was doing felt surreal. I felt as though I was experiencing vicariously my own existence; I felt like a visitor in my own life. Thoughts didn't register in my memory, I felt extremely impulsive at times, had difficulty filtering strange thoughts, and I became volatile. Sometimes I could hold thoughts well while there were other times I couldn't hold them much at all. My emotions oscillated from the extreme adrenaline rush of mania to the affliction previously described; and equilibrium was a concept and state of being which simply didn't exist for me much during this time. Many of my delusional thoughts became precepts and mainstays of my philosophy such as my belief in clichés and perfectionism. The delusions accumulated because of my inability to think rationally.

Years of psychological issues which I had never addressed were also working against me. I had never spoken to anyone about my middle school depression; suicide contemplation, the teasing, meaninglessness and derision I had undergone throughout high school, my fraternity experience, the cuts on my forearms. I searched for answers without any guidance and arrived at extremely delusional misconceptions, blaming my family and friends for my suffering. Searching for answers is great but I wasn't finding the right ones because my mind was poorly developed and I had no guidance.

I had never given much thought to my actions when I was younger and as I grew older I had merely been doing things out of habit rather than understanding why I did them. I usually looked to my companions to see what they were doing and copied their actions rather than thinking what the best course of action for myself would be. Sometimes I would hear my friends' words and act in a way which I felt would be in accordance with their thoughts. Many times, I would copy other peoples' actions without consciously thinking. This was a direct result of having a nebulous consciousness and being unable to process and create language to think my way through my day.

I knew most people surrounding me were able to think and make decisions with clarity throughout their lives and I felt plagued by my inability to do so and I tried as much as possible to develop my mind. I felt this was the cause of all my troubles—and it definitely was a contributing factor. I linked this practice of imitating others to all the stress, despair, and melancholy I had ever experienced, so I sought to break away from convention and find some answers of my own.

I previously lacked the foresight to see the consequences of actions; I was just beginning to consciously develop cause-and-effect thinking and spent a great deal of time thinking everything through. I was extremely concerned with thinking before acting and with knowing the cause and effect of any action before acting. I wanted a logical reason for every action and tried to figure out my world and develop my logical reasoning so I could think through situations. I knew there was some sort of logic in my new opinions, delusional thoughts, and beliefs. Unfortunately, the fact that I had some sort of logic—rather than the right logic—backing my actions created strong adherence to them. The strong emotional connections to righteousness and wrong-doing established earlier motivated me to deter-mine the consequences of every action.

My years of conformity left me with an ego boundary that was nebulous at best. The ego boundary is the boundary you develop in your personality be-tween yourself and others and is the barrier which states "I am different than other people" and helps you to make decisions independently instead of feeling compelled to copy the behavior of others surrounding you. I had such a lack of ego boundary when I was younger that many times I would repeat what others had said in brief blips, simply rephrasing other peoples' words and contributing very little original thought to conversations. F. Scott Fitzgerald once said "If you don't stand for anything the current will take you." That is exactly the image I formed of my younger self. I had never developed a philosophy with a mainstay of val-ues, precepts, and good habits; all I had to go by was a desire to fit in, so I had difficulty deciding what the right course of action should be in many situations. I was someone who constantly looked outside myself for di-rection. I knew I needed to develop a philosophy to so-lidify my values and personality. I was like an amor-phous blob that was constantly changing; I wanted to crystallize into a person of virtuous values who knew his own personality and then remain forever solidified in my own mold. I wanted to be my own person.

During the end of that summer I decided to isolate myself from everyone I knew so I could have the freedom to create and develop a personal philosophy. Up until this point there had been many people constantly trying to inform me what to do and how to be. This created a lot of confusion because their words weren't always exact, some of their thoughts were delusional, and many of their values conflicted. That is what led to my remaining silent when people stated things I disagreed with, because I thought any type of mental assent towards a value I disagreed with would condition my mind to believe in that value and corrupt me.

I also began double- and triple-checking everything I was doing. Part of this was because I felt I needed to ensure that my actions were perfect but another part was that I wanted to consciously ensure I had completed the action I was performing. Prior to then racing thoughts had prevented me from living in the moment so I was usually only partially aware of what I was doing. I was attempting to eliminate my previous spaciness and I felt I had to redo everything until I consciously registered whether it had been done — only this practice would keep me consciously in the moment. I used my thoughts to narrate my actions before performing them; if I did something before thinking it through, I would redo it a second time while attempting to think my way completely through the action.

I had routines which I absolutely had to perfect; otherwise I felt compelled to redo them. I felt if I skipped a step in a routine it would create poor mental conditioning. Having lived quite precariously for the past couple of years, I thought punctiliously routinizing my life would create stability, ignoring the fact that human error is a part of life and having mental flexibility is a great way to account for it. I thought if I made any mistakes my old way of living would somehow return to me with its accompanying pain and resentment. That fear motivated me to be as perfect as possible. I also felt adrenaline rushes while doing everything perfectly— another motivation to continue perfecting my actions.

During my morning routine I would eat breakfast, brush my teeth— first, top row then bottom—then shave, then wash my face. If for some reason I was inattentive and shaved and washed my face first I would start over by re-brushing my teeth then re-washing my face. The reason I brushed first is because I felt I wanted to take care of my insides before my outsides. If my face was already shaved and washed it didn't need to be shaved and washed twice and all I needed to do was brush my teeth after. I wanted to do things perfectly from the start and thought if I didn't there would be trouble.

The only how-to plan for living that has ever worked for me has been to make the best decision I can given the circumstances of my situation. Making mistakes is a part of being human, and as long as they are honest mistakes they are usually all right. I wasn't considering the purpose for my actions, which was getting ready for the day, and I didn't realize that if I had already made progress towards that goal it was detrimental to repeat the action for the sake of mental conditioning.

I thought about what I needed to do in order to live perfectly, and philosophized about how I could fix the world's problems. I was working at a transfer station and went on weekly trips to collect recyclables around town. I decided that I needed to start recycling everything that held no utility in the world. I believed the world was in dire condition and needed every last resource that could be obtained. I had accumulated a great deal of junk so I started sifting through everything I owned and recycling as much of it as I possibly could.

I had a TV, VCR, DVD player, sound system, and many other small items, but because they were all made in non-fair-trade countries, I thought the only righteous thing I could do was to recycle and replace them with items which were made in fair labor conditions. So I began this process. I thought as long as I used the non-fair-trade items I was creating and perpetuating the misery of millions of people overseas (when in fact I wasn't). Many items required disassembling. My tool set was comprised of all fair-trade items: a pocket knife, screw driver, and pry bar. I spent hours on the floor of my apartment at night disassembling as many of these items as I could. I stayed up until 2:00 or 3:00 AM every night and usually awoke for work around 6:00 AM.

During the entirety of this episode I felt mania rushing through me and I thought this was happening because I was being virtuous. Being virtuous can create happiness because it creates positive self-esteem, but I was unaware I had passed the point of optimal utility in my righteousness and was actually acting detrimentally. The adrenaline from mania helped keep me awake throughout this part of the episode. I slept about three to four hours a night.

I initially attempted to recycle all clothing bought in non-fair-trade countries but decided I would donate it back to the countries it came from, because the people who would receive it were probably the ones who originally manufactured it and deserved the fruits of their non-fair-trade labor. This left me with a very limited wardrobe which consisted of 3 pairs of pants and several shirts from work, which is all I wore. I also believed in the organic movement and bio-diversity and thought I needed to support both fair trade and organic clothing, so I began scouring the internet for clothes meeting both these criteria.

I then realized that my soap supply was not organic and stopped showering all together for two weeks because I felt if I didn't shower there would be more fresh water for others and no one would die of thirst. There is plenty of water in the world to go around; I was unaware that the people who did lack water lacked the means of obtaining and purifying it. I eventually went back to showering. I searched for fair trade items and remembered reading how the Greeks bathed with olive oil in the *Iliad* so I used that until I found a fair-trade organic soap I could wash with. I decided I could eat only organic foods, and also became vegan, because I believed the animals had just as much right to live as we did. In the grocery stores there weren't many nuts grown in the US, so I only ate peanut butter as my main source of protein because of its origin and price. I didn't have any cooking utensils so eggs were out of the question. I also didn't have a microwave so I ate bread with mostly raw vegetables and lost my ability to hold any food and began using the bathroom frequently. I would usually defecate at least twice a day and this contributed to weight loss.

I adopted the belief that physical objects in my life transcended the material world and attained intellectual standing in my mind, and that they comprised a piece of my personality. I thought as long as I kept items that represented or expressed bad values, they would forever remain a part of my subconscious and I would never be able to change my personality. I also thought that I could clear space in my mind by eliminating any superfluous physical items and the added mental space would facilitate my thinking. I sought to remove anything and everything which was excess in my life. I was expecting my stream of consciousness to improve after every recycling trip I took. I donated all my old jerseys, uniforms, children's clothes, shoes, and cleats and also recycled old sports posters. I still felt confusion in my values and personality and still felt I needed to completely change who I was. I organized my room as well as possible, thinking it would help me organize my mind.

My room was my recycling center and was organized into piles of different types of recyclables. I had a pile for plastics, a pile for electronic switch boards, piles for wiring, paper and cardboard, glass, and every other type of recyclable I had. Everything was on the floor because the apartment had no furniture. The piles surrounded one central spot in the bedroom which was my spot to sit while taking assembled items from one spot, disassembling them, and sorting the pieces into their respective piles.

One night that summer I was thinking about when my rent was due and realized it was due the very next day. It was about quarter to eight and I decided that, in order "to stay in propriety" and make the payment on time, I needed to drive to the landlord's office and drop off the check right away. I knew the landlord's office was far away and wasn't exactly certain how long it would take to get there. I found directions online and saw that I would be driving for quite a while, but decided I had to do this in order to maintain my end of the bargain. It took me six hours of highway driving to get there, and when I finally arrived I was at the wrong address. I knew I was in the right town because I saw a welcome sign that stated the town name I had been looking for, but this address definitely wasn't a real estate agency's. Not finding what I needed, I turned around and drove six hours back home that night, arriving in town around 8:30 am. I called called in sick to work while driving to my apartment and once I arrived I proceeded to the post office to drop the check in the mail, hoping I would still have an apartment after the late payment.

This is a good time to note that in the aftermath of the illness I was able to see how precarious the situation was but make light of it. It's possible for me now to look back and laugh about experiences like these. It's been helpful to have a good sense of humor about experiences like these because it helps me change my perception of them. I like to joke that I can mention this particular story if I'm applying for an apartment, to give the landlord a sense of how great a tenant I would be. When I can find humor in situations like these, experiences that were once negative become positive because I am able to laugh whenever I remember them. Who in their right mind drives 12 hours in the middle of the night with work and school the next day to pay the rent that only would have been a few days late had it been sent in the mail?

I eventually began thinking my mania was supernatural and that I was an agent of divinity and had to do everything perfectly in order to save the world. I thought that people would pick up on my habits, and then others would pick up from them the habits they had learned from me. Eventually this branching out of my original idea would pervade the world and change it. I was tenacious and had an extreme discipline which enabled me to do anything. I knew some of the habits I had adopted were strange and the clothes I was wearing were ragged but persisted because I thought I must make sacrifices for the world's survival and prosperity.

Another night there was a fire in the kitchen of the convenience store below my apartment and I awoke to the wailing of the fire alarm. I later interpreted the fire as an attempt on my life by some evil force that was attempting to prevent me from fulfilling my mission. The apartment next to me had a hole burnt through the floor and this was disconcerting because I always slept on the floor and realized that if I was one apartment over I could have been badly burnt. I overheard the fireman's and proprietor's conversation the next morning and they stated that the fire had started around 2:00 or 3:00 am, which was well after the convenient store closed, and they were relatively uncertain how it started. I now believe it was caused by grease, but at the time I believed someone attempted to kill me by throwing a cigarette into the kitchen through a small ventilation shaft on the first floor, hoping the building would catch fire and I wouldn't get out. The ventilation shaft probably had a screen over it to prevent bugs from flying into the kitchen, which means a cigarette couldn't possibly get through. I never concluded that if someone who really wanted to kill me could have found a much easier way than to throw a cigarette into a kitchen below my apartment and hope I wouldn't make it out. This speaks volumes to my ability to logically reason at the time.

The next semester began and I went to classes having only bathed with olive oil; I had developed a strange odor that created distance between myself and my classmates. My English classes were just as interesting as they had been. I also enrolled in Introduction to Existentialism. I didn't miss one class the entire semester. I began to adhere strongly to the philosophy I was learning, though I didn't fully understand it. Existentialism states that the meaning we find in life derives from the meaning we assign to our experience. I decided every action I took had to be extremely significant for my life to be meaningful, so I tried making everything as significant as possible. I believed every breath I was taking, and every step I completed during a walk were crucial moments in the day. This delusion slowed my already painstakingly slow execution of everyday actions and it only corroborated my belief that I needed to double-check every single thing I did to ensure it was done correctly.

During and after my episodes I was very adamant in my attention to detail and my belief that every detail was essential to living well. I still do pay attention to detail but now understand the consequences of some actions are far smaller than the consequences of others. This means little mistakes are perfectly all right to make because the consequences of them are usually harmless and they are also fairly easy to fix. I was concerned if I made even the slightest of mistakes it would somehow make me a bad person and lead to awful things. I have made many mistakes, little ones and some more significant ones, but I've learned from them, and I am still a good person who has not been corrupted by his mistakes. My doctor has always pointed out that mistakes are essential for growth and they help us create a course for our lives. Without mistakes, it would be pretty difficult to learn and we wouldn't be able to improve. It's also important to note it's human to make mistakes and not a single person on this earth ever has been or ever will be perfect. Understanding that mistakes are a part of life, has substantially decreased the number of mistakes I make, because having room for error has taken a lot of pressure off. Though I want to do my best, I realize that I can fix something if I need to, or just dismiss a mistake because the consequences of it are completely insignificant. A lot of times mistakes are also pretty funny and a good source of humor.

In English class we read mostly fiction, and I began interpreting everything in real life metaphorically. I could be talking with someone and as I turned to go up the stairs he might say, "Going up stairs now?" — I would reply "Yes," but internally I thought of my moving up the stairs as an ascendance in life. If I asked someone where a building on campus was and they say told me, "It's on the way," I might think of "the way" as the right way of being and associate this building with goodness, even though "on the way" was only intended directionally rather than morally and spiritually.

I was constantly searching for philosophic stability; if someone suggested crossing to the other side of the road, I took what had been said as an indication that I was on the right way to where I wanted to be in life. I began searching for deeper meaning and metaphor in everything everyone was saying. There is a great deal of ambiguity in language and many times metaphors can be created unintentionally. Hemingway stated that while writing he would create scenes without intending to put metaphor in them but his readers would perceive it anyways. If you begin searching for metaphors in life they can be fairly easy to find. The problem was that I was looking too deeply into what people were saying and missing their intended meaning because I was searching for deeper meaning. I thought everything that happened was some sort of sign, there to inform me whether or not I was being righteous at that particular moment, and whether I was headed the right way to obtain the stability I was searching for. Or the metaphor was helping me to fulfill my duty as an agent of divinity.

School work was consuming tons of my time. I was given large volumes of reading to do and my reading ability was inadequate. I spent a great deal of time researching and memorizing vocabulary. Meanwhile I wasn't retaining as much information as I needed to. While reading I extended my mind past its limits. After reading a certain number of hours, people usually need to rest or to call it a day because their minds simply can't process anymore. I was constantly extending myself beyond my limits and it created a breakdown in my thought processing, but I still forced myself to continue working, which created an extreme lightheadedness. It almost felt as though part of my brain simply turned off and from then on, my ability to register information was non-existent. I was reading words but wasn't obtaining much information from them. I had difficulty connecting parts of the sentences with other parts. I could physically feel my brain's inability to reason through situations. I was still obtaining passing grades of C plusses and B minuses, though most of the information I gained was from class discussion. My teachers caught on that something was wrong and one mentioned at the end of the semester that he thought I had a drug addiction.

I was still spending hours on the internet searching for clothing and I found two very light organic hemp hooded sweatshirts. From then on, I wore only the two of these. I couldn't find any socks, but I found organic underwear and also bought three organic t-shirts which I rotated regularly. My pants had been made in the US and I decided it would be all right to wear these until they needed replacing but I only had three pairs of pants. I did laundry weekly but didn't have any clothes to sleep in; I was wearing the same clothes I had on that day to bed and only changed all my clothes three times a week. I eventually found a pair of shoes that were organic and fair trade and replaced my comfortable work boots with these because they met my criterion for righteous clothing. They were poorly insulated and my feet were very cold; I could feel the pavement under my feet as I walked. The soles were so thin it was close to walking bare foot.

I never went to sleep until late because I wanted to spend time disassembling old items, which I would deliver to the transfer station as soon as I had accumulated enough material to merit a trip. I was still sleeping on the floor with no pillow and only one throw blanket, which fortuitously was made in the US but was very thin and provided little warmth. The tiles were cold, but I found that some tiles were actually softer than others and rested my head on these ones. I usually slept in my kitchen because the heater was located there, but I kept the heat as low as possible because I thought I needed to save energy to reduce ozone depletion. At nights, I kept the heat at 55 degrees Fahrenheit, though with the drafts and cold air it was probably more like 45. At one point my landlord complained that the pipes were freezing and told me I needed to always keep the heat on at least 65. After being spoken to, I turned the heat up to about 57 degrees.

I went from the beginning of August to almost mid October without a haircut and my hair got very long. I was afraid the clippers in the shop were non-fair trade and didn't want to allow a barber to use them to cut my hair. I allowed my hair to stand straight up because I thought it looked intelligent. One of my teachers sent me a message by cutting his hair a week after cutting it initially and hinting that he was all right after getting it cut. I went to the barbershop and had my head shaved.

I made it my dietary habit to eat only exactly what I needed to function. I thought if I ate less there would be more food in the world, and this would help feed the famished. I was making the same mistake in the way I thought about the food supply as I had made in regards to the water supply. There is actually plenty of food for everyone to eat them their fill. Famine is caused partly by corruption, partly by economic mismanagement, and partly by food spoilage; it has nothing to do with the amount of food in the world.

Hunger can keep anyone awake for any period of time and that was another reason why I was up so late at night. When I did fall asleep it was out of pure exhaustion and my body shut down for the two or three hours I slept. There were many nights I pissed myself because my mind simply wouldn't wake me to get up and use the bathroom. When I first changed eating habits in August I weighed about 190 lbs but at this point I was about 145 lbs. Part of my weight loss was muscle loss from no longer working out, but I am 5'9" and at that age should have weighed about 185 lbs, if in good health. Being famished also makes thinking far more difficult because you lack the energy and vitality to sustain substantive thoughts. My stomach felt like an enlarged hollow. The feeling of hunger which never left my body also distracted my mind. I was usually busy thinking and completing school work, but regardless of how immersed I became in my studies and reverie, part of my consciousness was almost always focused on my stomach.

For months, I avoided mirrors because I thought my vanity had created problems for me. I used to evaluate people by their looks rather than by their actions or the thoughts they expressed. I wondered if my shallowness was the reason I'd been made fun of so much. I decided that thinking about appearance was a distraction. I would concern myself only with functionality. I hadn't looked in the mirror for months and when I did—after my haircut that October—I barely recognized myself. My cheek bones were clearly defined and my skin was stretched thin across my jawline, leaving small hollows where my cheeks had been. My eyes were sunk deep and had large circles under them. I had previously filled out extra large hooded sweat shirts and was now swimming in a medium which ran small for mediums. My frame was once broad and muscular but now my shoulders were narrow and I could touch my thumb to my middle finger about four inches up my forearm. I could see parts of my rib cage in the center of my and it was clearly defined along my sides. My stomach was completely flat.

Studying, recycling, and not eating, I continued to feel the adrenaline from mania rushing through my veins. I read for hours and was so distracted by my emotions that I would focus more on generating the emotion than actually deriving information from the reading. I sometimes laid on the floor while recycling and felt complete exhaustion but forced myself to persist, fueled by adrenaline.

During the week, I started class around 8 am, went home and ate, and attended my second class for the day; I was done around 11 am. After that I made my way back to my apartment and spent about an hour or so thinking about what I would be doing for the rest of the day and ruminating over any other topic that came to mind. This was when I developed new delusions, such as not cutting my hair and thinking of my physical possessions as facets of my personality. I then went to the library where I would find an isolated cubby on the second or third floor and read for hours. The reading was usually 90 pages per class; at most I would have two classes worth in one day which should have taken me about five hours but instead took nine to ten hours because of exhaustion. After completing my school work I would go home and work on disassembling and recycling old possessions. I was still working outside of school until I realized I didn't have enough time to work and complete all my school work. I quit my job that October and focused primarily on school.

I began thinking that everyone was telepathic and could hear everything I was thinking, but I knew I couldn't hear what they were thinking. Sometimes I strained to hear their thoughts, which obviously I was unable to do. Eventually I decided to stop trying, out of respect for other people's privacy. I thought my thoughts were being broadcast on a secret telepathic network that everyone was listening to but I couldn't hear. I was waiting to eventually break through to this secret network and communicate telepathically. I wondered why people even spoke at all if they could communicate telepathically, eventually concluding that they spoke aloud because they knew *I* couldn't hear their thoughts without speech. This corroborated my belief that I was an agent of divinity and was the only person who had the power to save the world. It made me think that, once my powers were commensurate with everyone else's, I would be in a comfortable place in life. I became very self-conscious of my thoughts and felt I had to constantly think the right things because everyone would hear what I was thinking. I was embarrassed if my thoughts were in the wrong and felt the afflicted feeling previously mentioned.

A person who is experiencing a schizoaffective episode cannot differentiate between what is external and what is internal. During my own episodes, there seemed to be no boundary between my inner being and the world around me. I believed things happening outside of me had direct correlations to my thinking and my mind. Many of my beliefs at the time reflected this, such as my belief in the telepathic network or my belief that my possessions had standing and substance within the functionality of my consciousness.

I also began believing in telepathy because people generally intuit what you are thinking just by reading your facial expressions or by interpreting gestures. I was very unperceptive and unaware of the many ways people can determine someone else's thoughts. Sometimes I assumed teachers like the one who hinted at a hair cut could read my thoughts because that would explain how he knew I was afraid to get a hair cut. It's quite obvious that the teacher noticed my hair was ragged and overgrown and he probably just thought it would be a good idea to get a cut. I thought he must have known what I was thinking when in reality he was processing what was in front of him.

There were a few occurrences like this in class that fostered my belief in telepathy but they were mostly a result of teachers being observant and intuitive and also knowing I was listening to their every word. There were many occurrences of this nature where people naturally deduced what I was thinking from reading body language and thinking about the situation. I never made the connection. My facial expressions were quite demonstrative of my thoughts and I was unaware of this. For example, if someone were to cut in front of me while I was debating whether to go in line I might look somewhat perturbed. Another person might say, "I would have been mad too if I was cut, but oh well." While I was in fact angry that the person cut me, and evinced this through my facial expressions and body language, I thought the person making the remark had directly read my mind, not that he'd simply used logical reasoning to deduce what I was thinking.

I also thought because everyone else was tele-pathic, they all knew I was the only person who could save the world, that I was the spark plug that would in-fuse the world with the ideas it needed to bring every-thing to a state of righteousness. My belief that I was an agent of divinity stemmed from the idea that everyone has a predetermined purpose in life. In reality we make our lives the way we want them to be and develop a purpose in life by deciding what we want to do and how we want to impact our world. The character traits that lead to our decisions about what we want to do are de-veloped as a result of our experiences which create affinities towards certain activities. So, someone could be praised for writing well at a young age and continue to write throughout their adolescence because of this praise, thus developing an affinity towards the practice; that person might then decide to become a writer. The desire to write stemmed from the experience of getting positive feedback from writing; the continued pursuit of writing was a decision perpetuated by a positive psychological experience. Another person might consciously think about making a difference in the world and decide to pursue writing with the foreknowledge of its power. People develop their skills and abilities according to their proclivities. People are not predestined to become who they are; they consciously or impulsively make decisions that shape their lives. There are habitual thinkers and there are creative thinkers. Habitual thinkers may find this concept more difficult to believe because they allow their habits to control their actions while creative thinkers understand they are making conscious decisions to complete tasks—which makes this concept lucid. If you are a slave to your habits—as I was at an earlier age—you might find it difficult to believe no one is controlling you. At this point in my life my thinking was somewhere in between habitual and creative; I still believed I lacked complete control over my life. It took me a while to finally realize I had control over my own life.

In class I participated as frequently as possible but my speech was becoming unintelligible. I would utter snippets of information, which in my own mind made perfect sense because they were parts of thoughts I was thinking. Everyone else who had no idea what I was thinking only heard the snippets and was somewhat confused. My mind jumped from one idea to another and my thoughts moved so quickly that words I should have been saying later in the sentence came out before I'd spoken the preceding words. If the sentence was "I am going to study because I have an exam tomorrow," I might say "I… going…because exam." I think one of the most difficult things about schizoaffective disorder is losing your ability to communicate. I had the ideas sitting in an un-verbalized form in my conscious mind but couldn't formulate them into coherent sentences while experiencing psychosis. I also still thought people should understand what I was saying because the ideas made sense in my mind at the time. Besides, people were supposed to be telepathic.

While attempting to communicate, I assumed people had foreknowledge of the ideas I wanted to express and I only needed to mention them as if we had already had a conversation about them. The conversation could be about existentialism and the teacher might reference a desk and state, "There is no certainty whether the desk will be here once I return." I simultaneously could have been thinking about how I misplaced something at home—my computer, for instance— and found it in another place later. I would blurt out in mid-conversation, "What about the computer?" In that classroom, there were clearly no computers. Most people began dismissing the things I said, because they knew something was clearly wrong. The teacher would advance the lecture forward by giving some assent such as "okay" or "all right". This happened frequently because I was too much inside my own mind and had difficulty discerning the internal from the external, but also because I thought people were telepathic and already knew what I was going to say from having listened to my thoughts. I believed I only had to reference a thought and they would know what I meant.

Also, I was so accustomed to thinking in isolation and carrying on conversations with myself that when I spoke aloud, what I said was often a continuation of that internal monologue. Obviously, no one had any of the background that supported the strange spoken snippets of thoughts which were taken out of the context of my internal monologue and posited randomly into external dialogue.

Another facet of my incoherence correlates to the nature of conscious thought. Sometimes conscious thought is generated in snippets, several words, and/or sentence fragments rather than complete sentences; it isn't always hashed out the way someone would do if they were talking to someone else. I spoke the way I thought. I attribute this to my isolation and to my inability to discern the external from the internal. If every conscious thought was a complete sentence then these snippets would have been complete sentences and it would have been far easier to understand me. The ability to change thoughts into coherent language was completely absent for me during my episodes.

For example, the complete expression of one of my thoughts might have been, "I have to leave at quarter after four, eat at 4:30, and leave for class at 5:10," but I might have said to myself, "Okay, leave at quarter after 4, food 4:30, leave for class by 5:10." This example is actually a more complete sentence than I would generally use, but the point is that a lot of the words we would use in conversation are skipped when we are thinking to ourselves, because the thinker knows the subject matter and makes presumptions that would need to be communicated if the thought were expressed to someone else. My thoughts started from the raw stage where there were only snippets of information and were spoken in this format. If during an episode, I continued speaking aloud as if I was still in my internal monologue, I might have said something like "4:30, the food, class"—my listener would have no definitive understanding of the information I was trying to communicate.

I eked out thoughts and snippets of thoughts partially because I was unable to create coherent language but also because I was afraid of the disapproval I may receive from others. During my episodes I lost the courage to open up and speak to people because I was afraid people were judging me; I was afraid they would express their disapproval in a negative way, or they would not respond at all. They might turn away in silence, as I had turned away from people I thought were un-genuine. I lacked the reassurance that my words would responded to tactfully; this created a self-consciousness that arrested some of my speech. Having ignored others, I now found myself unable to communicate with people. Many people probably didn't want to say much to me because they were afraid of being around me. I was in a state of psychosis and it showed in my thoughts, actions, and appearance. It was evident something was wrong and the less they interacted with me the better off they thought they would be.

Referential thinking also played havoc with my ability to communicate. I thought life was an allegory; it was my responsibility to interpret what people were saying and react accordingly. My belief in the cliché that "everything happens for a reason" led me to believe there were no coincidences. There is plenty of random information passing through our consciousness daily that is completely disconnected to other occurrences in our lives. Unfortunately, I interpreted every detail as if it had meaning and felt I needed to fully understand everything in order to make the right decisions. If I was trying to decide what my next action would be and decided in favor of one option and shortly thereafter heard someone say the word "good" or "great" just in passing and without any direct reference to me, I believed that meant I had a good or great idea in mind. I would proceed to implement the idea. If someone I wasn't talking to were to say "the grass is always greener on the other side" I'd interpret it as a sign that I was in the right place. I sometimes took the occasion to reflect on how good I thought my life was.

Conversely, if I heard negativity in other people's conversations I would stop and wonder if I was doing things correctly. If I heard a siren off in the distance from a fire truck or ambulance, I became worried that something bad was going to happen in my own life and I thought through whether I was in the wrong. If I heard the word "no" or someone in passing saying something like "that's not my favorite," I applied it to my own life and stopped to think through everything I was doing.

Sometimes I would stop to think whether I had accomplished everything I needed to for the day thus far. I thought through whether homework assignments had been completed, errands had been run, groceries were in my house, my car was correctly parked, and determined whether there was anything else that needed disassembling. If I was walking to a particular place, hearing negativity might stop me in my tracks; I would ruminate over whether I needed to go back to my apartment and fix something or whether I needed to continue forward. I would start to make a decision and would walk a few paces towards the apartment then turn back a few paces in the direction I was originally going. My memory was sluggish from sleeplessness and psychosis and I felt I needed signs and clues to remind me of what I needed to do.

If I were thinking about filling up my car's gas tank and heard someone say "I'm full" (referring, of course, to his own stomach), I interpreted it as a sign that I should go and fill the gas tank. I'd listen for signs like these and interpret them as hints in determining my next course of action. My mind was so worn out at this point that I was unable to make decisions after logically weighing my options; I was searching for help outside myself.

I knew at the time that my life was in a bad way. During one of my Existentialism classes, my professor was talking about how Jean Paul Sartre taught existentialism while imprisoned during World War Two. I directly equated Sartre's experience to my own feeling of imprisonment. I felt trapped, immobilized mentally, and confused. Being unable to think rationally is extremely burdensome and disconcerting. On top of that, I was unable to coherently verbalize any of my thoughts. Being unable to communicate is extremely isolating. One of the most frequent ways people make connections is through conversation and I was unable to speak or interpret language coherently. Plus, I had very little opportunity to converse because most people were afraid to interact with me. I was isolated. The Sartre reference seemed directly related to my situation. I took it as advice to talk more with people and teach them about what I was thinking in order to liberate myself. When I did communicate with others it was definitely helpful, even though I wasn't making much sense, because I felt I was making some sort of connection. These short periodic conversations made me feel good.

I picked up other pieces of philosophy and logic in class and thought the teachers were directly relating the literature to my life. They knew something was wrong, and they knew I was listening, so they gave me some hints of advice, which was helpful and kept me going. I thought they were speaking directly to me when in reality their lesson plans were structured so students could learn about life from the literature. My professors talked about the power of literature and how important it is to convey information. I thought, "If there is one place I could make a difference in life, it could be as a writer."

I began believing I needed to become a writer in order to save humanity by disseminating all the lessons I had learned. I felt I had to expose everyone else to their demons and tried doing so by evaluating personalities and then making comments that I thought would be helpful to classmates. During a presentation, I specifically referenced situations I felt specific people in class could learn from and talked about morals in hopes it would help other people change. Most of the people didn't have problems like mine, but I felt that many people would soon experience the enlightenment I was going through and would change for the better. One of my classmates who was scheduled to present with me intentionally misplaced the notes I had created, which I was going to use to discuss issues related to the personal problems I interpreted people as having. Unfortunately, I remembered all of my conversation points and the the page numbers of my references. The presentation was quite awkward.

One time I considered living entirely off the land in the wilderness in complete isolation and leaving everyone and everything I knew behind. I eventually decided against it because I thought my leaving would be turning my back on the world's problems when I thought I had so many solutions. I felt the adrenaline of mania throughout the day and into the night until the very moment I fell asleep. I thought it was a direct result of my actions. What is disconcerting is that even today I still get that adrenaline feeling if I start thinking about it, though now I can rid myself of it by focusing my mind on other things.

At the time of my episodes, I considered mania a supernatural occurrence brought about by righteousness. Now I think the release of adrenaline was a de-stressing mechanism, a way to counter the stress I felt from trauma, sleeplessness and isolation. It was triggered by the positive association I had formed between the idea of "righteous action" and the feeling of mania. I was under the illusion this adrenaline feeling was created when everything in my life was as it should be, when my thoughts were pure and my actions were in accordance with the purity of my thinking. I gave no thought whatsoever to the utility of my actions, so long as they came of what I considered "pure" intentions. (These days, I do what actually needs to be done, without thinking too much about purity.)

I wanted to help everyone feel this way. I thought if they became perfectionists like myself, they too could have this feeling, which in turn would create a golden age. Calling to mind the ancient Chinese dynasties, I thought about how to initiate this golden age. I concluded that the only way for me to help everyone achieve this end was by continuing to perfect everything I was doing; everyone else would learn from my actions rather than from me telling them. Unfortunately, my unwillingness to talk about my grandiose plans contributed to the diminishment of my health. If a family member had known the things I was thinking, they probably would have intervened much earlier.

I was also prey to darker thoughts. If I was working towards the correction of the world, there was a force that was working against me in secrecy. During my episodes, I was always suspicious of anyone and everyone near me and the few people who were still a part of my life, including my family; I wondered whether they had my best interest or some ulterior motive in mind. I trusted my professors mostly, because they sounded genuine and had sound logic. They were the only people I ever listened to.

While driving home to collect more possessions I could recycle, I noticed I was surrounded by a group of cars. This generally occurs when there is traffic, but I interpreted the arrangement of vehicles on the highway as a protective formation to guard me against evil do-ers. I thought the people who were surrounding my ve-hicle—and coincidentally driving at the exact same speed as I was—were there to protect me. This con-tributed to my foreboding, because if people needed to protect me, there had to be a reason! It also increased my feeling of self-importance.

Many of the delusions I suffered, like thinking I was a messiah, were a direct result of wanting to feel I was important to others. My greatest fear was isolation and I had become completely isolated; my condition made me unable to have positive social interactions. I dreamed of being lauded by everyone who had previ-ously ostracized and alienated me.

I wanted to believe all my suffering was happen-ing for a reason, that in the end it would produce an ex-traordinary amount of good that would make it all worth while. I worried that people held grudges against me for all the contentious interactions we'd had, but everything would be fixed and all the resentment would be forgiven if I completed my mission of saving the world. I day-dreamed of being reunited with people I had been completely out of touch with, who once were my friends.

I thought that a man who stood at the bus stop every day was waiting for me to pass by on my way to class so he could monitor me to ensure my well-being. (In reality the bus arrives at 8:00AM and my classes began at 8:00AM and the bus stop happened to be di-rectly on my way.) I looked for approval from him be-cause I thought he was concerned with my well-being. I nodded and sometimes waved and he responded out of respect, which is what most people would do, but I took this as a secret understanding that he was keeping watch for me. There were many instances where I passed people and exchanged everyday cordialities; I interpreted their gestures as acknowledgement that they had recognized the world's savior. They were nodding in assent to my mission.

I was constantly worried that there were people who were out to get me and I was ever vigilant. My eyes darted from person to person and I constantly looked over my shoulder to find out what people were doing. I felt anything could happen at any moment. I was skittish and sometimes I quickly stepped out of the way of anyone who might knock into me. I also took the longest strides possible because I thought I needed to make the most out of every step. This attracted some attention. I was dressed in a hemp sweatshirt with brown pants, a shaved head, and shoes that looked like Converse sneakers, and I carried a hemp organic bag, I would have stuck out even if I was sane. People could see the paranoia and worry on my face which in turn made them apprehensive. That created a situation where the only people I was interacting with were people who were on edge. People's apprehension about my physical state increased my own fear and anxiety, because I thought if they were afraid of something, then I should definitely be afraid too. I wasn't aware my appearance and demeanor was the reason for and the way people reacted to me. Knowing this would have been very helpful.

Sometimes when people looked at me with astonished perplexity, I interpreted their looks as an indication that these people realized they were seeing the next messiah—of course they were amazed! (This is something I like to laugh about now, especially after saying or doing something ridiculous). Sometimes I caught people looking at me that way and then they would make an effort to speak cordially to me, which made me think they were simply happy to see me—the *messiah*—in person.

Whenever I spoke with my parents, I would argue intensely over trivial matters, always suspecting them of attempting to control me. Sometimes they would call and try to persuade me to do something because they had my best interest in mind and wanted to ensure that I was going to make a good decision. They knew something was wrong but many of our conversations ended in me hanging up. I didn't want to be controlled in any way, shape, or form.

My mom was more objective than my dad and was better at presenting information and allowing her logic to convince people. My dad's method of persuasion was to create emotional cues which he expected would get people's assent to what he was saying. For that reason, I spoke with my mom and completely ignored and avoided my dad. In the one conversation I did have with my Dad, I accused him of creating facades. I thought his manner of creating emotional cues was his attempt to control me, when in fact that was his usual way of communicating with everyone. My parents sometimes thought that if they said something then I should feel obliged to listen, and I felt the need to protect my independence. Only later did I come to understand that, when people say things with the expectation for me to agree, I still always have the freedom to disagree if I feel like it.

It was so important to me not to feel persuaded into doing anything that I argued about semantics. If I had just spoken to my mom about something I might do, such as call her later in the week, she would say, "So you'll call me later this week?" and I would demand to know why this wasn't phrased in the form of a question. I was angry that she had made an assumption something I might or might not do. My mom would state, " So you're going to pay that bill, right" —and I would become angry that she'd attempted to obtain my assent to her agenda. Sometimes my reaction would be to tell myself, "I won't pay the bill," so I wouldn't feel obliged to pay it. "I will pay the bill later on." By restating it that way, I thought I was eliminating her persuasion from my mind and deciding on my next action independently. She really found it to be an obvious course of action which was the only reason she assumed I would pay it, but I wanted her to ask, "Are you going to pay the bill?" so I could make my own decision.

Whenever I was asked if I planned to do something, my response would always begin with "I might" or "I may." I thought saying the words "I will" would oblige me to do whatever I assented to do, denying me the option of changing my mind if I thought better of it. In short, I was searching for autonomy. At the time, I didn't realize that regardless of how someone words a question, whenever I am asked to do something, it is always my decision as to whether or not I will do it, which renders their wording or any persuasiveness unimportant. I can weigh the options and examine the logic of the decision and ultimately make decisions independently. At the time, though, I didn't want to make any verbal commitments, because whenever I did, I felt compelled to do exactly what I said I would do; I had to "be a person of my word" and felt people wouldn't value my word if I changed my mind. I thought I was liberating my mind by not formally committing to anything because non-commitment would free me to do whatever I wanted. I lacked the mental flexibility that would allow me to change my mind when necessary.

The easiest way to communicate with me during my schizoaffective episodes to be objective and allow me the illusion that I was completely in control of the interaction. Even in situations where the the decision to be made was obvious, an objective question or statement worked best. Almost always phrasing a request in question form and *asking* me to do something with as much objectivity in tone and voice as possible was the best way to get me to do anything. I had a good moral compass and wanted to do the right things but just didn't want someone else telling me what to do. I later grew out of this stubbornness after taking medication as I came to understand that I always have a decision as to my actions, regardless of what someone else says or does. Schizoaffective episodes are very disorienting experiences; I felt my life was completely precarious at the time and my demand for objective questions was part of my search for agency and mental independence.

I often used equivocal language to advance conversations. People sometimes asked, "You'll do that, right?" and I would reply "Okay," with the understanding that the word "okay" was equivocal. In my mind, I was thinking "Okay, I heard what you said," even while knowing that people would interpret my response as an assent to do something.

Later that November I took a trip home to find some new items I could recycle and spent the evening at home. I slept on the carpeted floor in my room and it was extremely comfortable and helped me sleep for a considerable time. I found a sleeping bag at home, which surprisingly and luckily enough was US made, and I decided to bring it back to my apartment at school. This helped a bit and I was able to sleep a little more comfortably, but I still kept myself up late at night because of the addiction to mania's adrenaline and also because I now felt compelled to become a writer who would save the world. Having learned that writing is the best way to disseminate information, I thought if I could articulate all my new values to everyone I would be able to create the golden age I had been dreaming of.

I was still recycling everything possible and this was coupled with a desire to create as much space as I possibly could. Before recycling a plastic bag, for example, I rolled it to compress it so it consumed the least amount of space possible and then crammed it into the recycling bag. I thought that I had to save space in the world and that my compaction of every item I recycled or threw away would also save space in my mind. I rolled everything I recycled as tightly as I possibly could; if the roll wasn't tight enough I started over and rolled until I thought it was as tight as it could be.

I class I experienced the adrenaline type feeling while listening to lectures. This emotion definitely showed, which is why one teacher probably thought I was on drugs. I breathed in and out very slowly and thought about the adrenaline feeling and focused on the experience of it. Sometimes I breathed in sharply after hearing an interesting point that I could adopt into my philosophy and ultimately disseminate to everyone; I was excited I had some new information that I thought could change the world. I started thinking about economy of breath and thought I should only use as much as air as I needed so there would be more air for other people and the earth wouldn't run out. Sometimes I ran out of breath after a long walk and had to stop to catch it, but I breathed in very slowly to feel the emotions and adrenaline. This is a good practice for catching one's breath, but my reason for doing so was irrational. There were many things I did that were seemingly normal and rational that lacked normal and rational reasoning behind them.

Although I wasn't eating much I tried to eat healthy. I never actually researched the the right serving amounts for all the food groups, but I ate what I thought was right and I was still losing weight.

My being alcohol free had improved my vision,

but, strange to say, schizoaffective disorder also improved my vision, immensely. The disorder has a way of sharpening your senses because of the adrenaline you feel throughout the day. The paranoia also improves your senses, because your body goes on a heightened alert when it believes there is danger present.   I was quite amazed at the clarity with which I was now seeing the world, and at the richness of color I perceived. I constantly looked at nature in awe. There were times I was stared out windows during class and marveled at the detail and beauty of the trees. My eyes widened and my adrenaline increased during these times. I changed my breathing and it was fairly audible, which contributed to my estrangement. We were in the middle of class and I was looking across the room out the window at trees while other students were listening to the lecture.

One day a professor read a passage from fiction that stated "it was like removing a layer of cellophane"— which described how I felt about my change in eyesight. I thought my eyesight had improved due to eating fair trade and organic foods; I considered anything non-fair-trade tainted and believed it would cause problems in my thinking and vision. I had experienced a change in vision and it did feel as though I had removed a layer of cellophane, which made me think the professor knew exactly what I was experiencing and was directly referencing it.

My decision-making ability continued to get worse. I vacillated between options, attempting to determine the best decision and wasting tons of time. I became so immersed in my deliberations that I was unaware of the hours I was wasting debating the best option for every decision. I found possible faults in each of the options I was weighing. My habitual fault-finding left me stuck between options. Sometimes I'd start walking in one direction and then change my mind and turn in the other direction and then switch again back to the original decision. At one point my philosophy professor stated that you had to make a decision one way or another—even if it's the wrong one— because otherwise you'll spend all your time thinking and will never accomplish anything. This was helpful to hear and my decision-making speed slightly improved.

It was early December and my referential thinking was at a point where I believed I needed guidance from external stimuli for almost every decision I made. I was making decisions according to what I overheard in other people's conversations. These were conversations that had nothing to do with me or anything I was thinking, but I picked out snippets and words that seemed to coincide with my thoughts at any particular moment. I even read people's gestures and body language as expressing approval or disapproval of my thoughts. I thought everything in life was interrelated and a part of one entire whole and was unable to distinguish a conversation I had nothing to do with from my internal monologue. I believed that regular actions in life were metaphors describing the nature of my life. Ascending a staircase in the library meant I was ascending in life by obtaining my education. It seemed as though everything happening outside of my conscious mind correlated with everything inside it.

I still thought everyone believed I was the one who would save the world. Referential thinking made me believe that I needed to throw a party and invite all my old friends who I hadn't spoken to in months. I believed everyone would be attending and I went to the grocery store in preparation, but had difficulty communicating what I needed. The store manager assigned a clerk to shop with me. We walked around the store and looked for items and she attempted to figure out what I needed. Sometimes I stared at items and would think I needed that item and ask, "Are you going to buy this?" I interpreted her questions as hints that I should buy these items and did. I began believing that people around me were often hinting at decisions I ought to make, because they knew I had to be successful in becoming a writer in order to save the world. I also believed the way I lived my life would carry over into my writing. The grocery trip left me with a medley of items, many of which I would never have eaten regularly, but I bought them anyways and proceeded home to put the food away.

I then decided I needed to exercise before the party I had been planning and I made a trip to the gym. I was wearing sweat pants which were 2 inches above my ankle bone, my organic hooded sweatshirt, and the thin Converse-like sneakers. Before leaving, I called people and told them how I was having a party. Many of the conversations I had were disjointed. Most people were kind but none were planning on attending, but I still kept calling and inviting people. Arriving at the gym, I asked the front desk attendant "Who should I invite?" without mentioning that I was throwing a party. I didn't even know her at all. I assumed she had the knowledge that I was throwing a party; at this point I believed everyone knew exactly what I was thinking at all times. I asked her multiple times what she thought and if she was going to attend and I paced back and forth in front of the check-in area debating what I should do. She called the campus police and I was put into protective custody. I was interviewed at their station and questioned as to whether I was on drugs. At the time, I was eating the herb salvia which I had picked up at the grocery store as a part of my regular diet, as I informed the officer, but he believed I was smoking—not eating—the herb. He never of course found any on me and eventually released me to the custody of a friend I hadn't spoken to for months, and I returned to my apartment.

There were many people out that night because it was the last day of classes before finals. Later that night I went to the fraternity I had belonged to, and started talking to people who were once my friends. I wasn't making much sense but it felt great to see them, and they could obviously tell from my demeanor, speech, and clothing that I was off. I was asked to leave, but then—through referential thinking—I got the idea that I was supposed to return to the fraternity, so I did. This happened three times. The idea came to me because I interpreted peoples' gestures towards one another as gestures for me to follow them, so I did. When I returned the fourth time, I was punched in the jaw by a guy I had wrestled nine months ago. I was confused by the incident. It was a cheap shot, taken while I was in conversation with someone else out on the front lawn, and my jaw hurt for a good week and a half. I left the house and then overheard someone saying, "You should get a whole pizza." At that point I was starved, and was elated to hear this news. I bought a large pizza and took it to my apartment and ate the whole of it.

Early the next morning I decided I needed more groceries in preparation for more guests and went to the store. I brought the car thinking there would be too much to carry, even though I lived only a hundred yards away. I began shopping, thinking deeply before choosing each item. People were looking at me perplexedly. At this point I weighed about 122 lbs, my clothes were dirty, and most people probably thought I was homeless. I was still skittish and was constantly looking around in paranoia, and I began observing what others were buying to determine what I needed for the party. People would look at me and then put an item in their cart. I began following shoppers thinking they were hinting at me to buy the exact same items as they were, and I did. I spent at least two hours shopping and purchased over $300 in groceries, most of which was produce. While checking out I called home to ask if I could use the credit card and my folks okayed it. At this point they knew they needed to intervene. Having interacted intermittently with me during my episode, they realized I had regressed to a state where I couldn't function properly.

I advise people who have loved ones who they believe are mentally ill to make an effort to visit that loved one and get them help before they decline to a state of being similar to what mine was at that time.

They told me they were coming to visit. I left the groceries in my car.

Chapter 3
First Hospitalization and Initial Therapy

We met at a local coffee shop where we ate breakfast and they asked that I leave with them because my sister was supposedly throwing a party that she wanted me to attend. I had previously thought they were working against me, but in a conversation earlier that day on the phone, they told me they were on my side. I began believing them because they genuinely did care for me and this was evident during our conversation. Hearing them tell me they were on my side completely changed my perception of them and I began to trust them again. They drove me to a regional hospital which housed a psychiatric unit instead of taking me to the psyche hospital which was much further away; they were afraid I would figure out what they were doing before we got there. When we got there, they convinced me I needed to check in to get well. I considered running but was uncertain of how far I'd get before being caught, and I didn't know the area very well. Part of me realized I needed some help, but I mostly signed the forms because I thought through referential thinking it was my responsibility to check in. I was kindly encouraged that this would be for the best. The nurse who conducted the initial interview informed me I could only be admitted to the hospital if I wanted to, and this definitely made things easier. I was afraid of being persuaded or manipulated into doing anything and if they did attempt to hospitalize me without my consent there might have been problems. There were some preliminary conversations; the doctors had to determine whether I needed to be there and decided I did.

During the first three days of this hospitalization I slept most of the time and was encouraged to eat as much as possible. I was prescribed sleeping medication

and anti-psychotics, which rid me of paranoia. .
and secure. The medication helped me relax and clai.
fied my thinking; I was more in control of my thoughts
than I had been previously, which was relieving. I was
regaining sanity but still had many delusional ideas.
The main reasons for my initial recovery were medication and the return of basic everyday comforts that had
been non-existent during my episode. The medication
made me hungry, returned some sanity to my mind, and
helped me sleep. I was encouraged to gain weight; this
was the first time in six months I had eaten a hot meal. I
usually ate about one and a half servings per sitting. I
was now sleeping on a mattress with a pillow instead of
on tiles. Having adequate bedding in a well-heated living space helped knock me out for hours. I slept so
long and so soundly that I wet the bed at least twice.
My parents brought the warm clothing I hadn't donated
yet. Wearing winter clothing and feeling warmth was
relaxing. Having warm feet was probably the most
memorable part because my feet had always been cold
and it felt incredible to have warm socks. My apartment
at school was frigid and the school buildings were fairly
cool too, because the heating system was old, so I was
constantly cold throughout this first episode. Everyone's
kindness also helped calm me. I began interacting with
other patients on the unit and it was the first time in
months that I carried on somewhat intelligible conversations. Many of the conversations were still disjointed but
I was connecting with people again. Sometimes I
laughed too. I hadn't been laughing much. There were
therapy groups where mental health topics were discussed, and I was encouraged to participate, but I only
wanted to sleep. I left my room for meals and free time.
　　I didn't think much about anything other than
sleeping, eating, and adapting to this new environment.
I was in a new wing of the hospital where the windows

were covered with tarps because the scaffolding was still attached to the sides of the building. This made the wing somewhat ominous. The nurses gave me ointments for my hands which were still cut up from my having over-washed them. The nurses also cured other small ailments which I had developed during the past six months.

During the day, I met with the main psychologist on the unit, who I didn't trust. He asked personal questions that I didn't want to answer. I felt embarrassed to reveal any personal information to someone I had just met. I also felt ashamed to admit there were problems in my life. He was intelligent and extremely concise but wasn't very personable. There was some caring in his voice but mostly he displayed an indifferent objectivity. I felt he was only interested in the information I might give him; he wasn't concerned for my well-being. I think I mistook his professionalism as indifference towards me and this made me less inclined to speak to him. I still think there is a way someone can objectively ask questions while still showing they care. Our conversations were strictly about my experience and his professionalism was somewhat chilling. My responses were terse because I was afraid to talk to him.

I had previously ignored all my problems and thought admitting them was a sign of weakness. I was accustomed to being made fun of for having even the smallest of problems so I usually kept quiet when something was wrong in order to avoid criticism. I ignored problems hoping they would go away, which never happened. Although they might be pushed from my consciousness, they were still existing in my subconscious and were hindering my well-being.

I felt answering some of the Doctor's questions would be complaining and didn't realize I could present information with the mindset of solving a problem rather

than lamenting over an issue. I had a negative perception of complaining because whenever I had complained in the past, it made me feel lame. Since learning to present information with the intention of resolving
an issue, I haven't felt I am burdening the doctor or being ungrateful. This has made me more willing to share
my issues with others. And sometimes it's acceptable to
lament over an issue.

Part of me felt other people would learn of my
issues and I would be humiliated when they did. I didn't
realize that doctors must maintain confidentiality and
that the only way anyone can learn anything about me
is if I tell them. It can be somewhat difficult to fully trust
in a doctor's confidentiality; it initially seemed unrealistic
to think that doctors wouldn't divulge secrets to others.
How often had I shared secrets with friends only to find
out that everyone knew them by the end of the school
day? I thought if I spoke too much about my illness,
people would somehow learn about it. The only way
anyone can learn anything about a patient is if the patient informs them. When doctors talk about patients to
other doctors or anyone else they usually withhold the
patient's name and simply call them a patient. Most
doctors are in medicine because they want to help
people, and they understand that divulging a patient's
personal information is detrimental to the patient's well-
being, and possibly their own.

Another facet of my inability to address an issue
and solve it was habitual. I was in the habit of ignoring
problems and acting as if everything was all right. I had
never addressed major issues in my life. Part of the
reason for my inclination to ignore problems was the
pain associated with these memories. I didn't want to
mentally revisit any parts of my life that had been
painful because of the emotions connected to them,
and I didn't understand why someone would ask me to

do so. I thought ignoring the issues would cause the pain to go away, and it does, temporarily. The sting of an emotion may be diminished for the moment by ignoring it, but there is still a negative emotional effect from leaving unaddressed issues nagging at your psyche. The problems I left unaddressed hampered me until I actually talked about them in therapy, which turned out to be quite liberating.

Being hospitalized and medicated, I was able to think with some sanity for the first time in years. I had lost all my friends and didn't know a single person outside my family who was going to talk to me, and I was in disbelief at my situation and didn't want anyone to know anything about my episode. I was concerned about all the times I had yelled at people and the contention I had created, and the coldness with which I had treated everyone. I didn't understand how I became that way. I felt robbed of all my friendships and of many good times I could have had over the past years, while instead I experienced the episode and the loss of everyone close to me except my family. It was a subject that continually re-entered my mind despite my trying to put it on the back burner.

During my stay in the hospital I ruminated over my losses and convinced myself I wouldn't be able to reconnect with my friends from college. I was depressed for as long as I thought about the loss of my old friends. I eventually realized I would have to try making new friends, which I did successfully in later years; I moved on and made new friends, and I enjoy their company to this day. They are people I get along with well because I sought their friendship, knowing we have similar values and are good people. But I only began making new friends once I left behind the experience of losing all my old friends during that first episode.

The hospitalization continued and I felt an overwhelming fear of being kept indefinitely. I had heard of people who were held in state hospitals for years and tortured and was growing increasingly apprehensive. While an in-patient, I was never told how long I would stay because the medical personnel were uncertain of how much time it would take to stabilize me. I sat wondering when I could leave and began feeling trapped. The windows were still covered by tarps and we were confined indoors. This contributed to my feeling of entrapment. I think we should have at least been chaperoned to walk around outside the building. I began thinking how I could get out and concluded that the only way I'd be going home was if I showed sanity. I began feigning sanity in every way I knew how. I stopped pacing the hallways and began acting in ways I thought were socially acceptable. I tried greeting people as I passed them in the halls, where I had previously ignored them. I answered every question with the response I knew the medical personnel were looking for, and acted in all the conventional ways that I figured were considered healthy or normal, (such as speaking when being spoken to).

During meetings with the head doctor I asked from time to time when I'd be leaving. I was curious to find out, but I didn't want to ask too often, because I was afraid if I did he would learn my goal was to leave as quickly as possible. He might feel compelled to keep me longer. The doctor always gave an indefinite answer, because he wanted to ensure I was released at the right time and didn't want to give any false expectations. I began to be suspicious that he was intentionally avoiding my questions and planning on keeping me indefinitely. I constantly worried about being allowed to leave. I felt I had created the appearance of sanity but I'm uncertain what the medical personnel believed. Internally I still felt unstable but knew I needed to project stability in order to get home. After nine days, I was finally released. One of the main factors was that it was late December and they were short on hospital beds.

Once I was home I celebrated a late Christmas with my family. I was overwhelmed with all the non-fair trade clothing they had bought me, but decided I needed some sort of clothing and accepted the gifts anyways. I checked the tags after opening the packaging and was disappointed, seeing the names of the countries labeled on them. But it was comforting being with family and returning home, where I had so many positive and relaxing memories. The house was warm and I didn't go out much. I was still in a precarious mental state and it showed in many of my actions. I stayed in my room most of the time and read the last Harry Potter book in two days. After doing so, I progressed to other books to prepare my mind for the upcoming semester. I was growing increasingly tired and somewhat depressed and the adrenaline type feeling was non-existent. Hunger and tiredness are side-effects of medication which for me contributed to oversleeping and overeating. I also felt lame from inactivity. I ran on the treadmill and still wore my organic hemp sweatshirt with sweat pants which only extended to mid-ankle while exercising. Sometimes I went into the garage and decided I needed to jump rope, but because my jump rope wasn't fair trade I practiced the motion of jumping rope without a rope.

After hospitalization, it took me several months to become cognitively functional. It's important to realize that it takes time to recover. F Scott Fitzgerald wrote in *Tender is the Night* that you have to overlook the negative occurrences of mental illness and "love your family members for their best selves. " The main character in this story has a wife with schizophrenia and in real life Fitzgerald's wife had schizophrenia. It takes time for people to get to their best states of being but it's important to stick with them and help them progress.

I had missed my finals the previous semester because of the hospitalization. My parents emailed my teachers informing them of what had happened and sent doctors notes as proof. I was allowed to complete two of the finals from home while the third teacher, who had kicked me out of his class that summer, denied my request to retake his final. I went to visit his office a couple of days before the beginning of the next semester and we talked about why I didn't take the final. I told him I had been in the hospital but he thought it was a ploy to buy more time to complete the work. He informed me that he thought I was on drugs the previous semester. He could obviously see I had gained weight, was well clothed, and was speaking coherently; he presumed I was lying about the hospitalization. He asked me why I was hospitalized but I didn't want to tell him because I was embarrassed about having schizoaffective disorder and didn't want anyone knowing. I replied again in despair that I was hospitalized, afraid that he wouldn't believe me, and he didn't. He thought that he'd found a fallacy in my argument, which was my not having a particular reason for being hospitalized. I don't tell most people about my illness, but this was a private conversation, and I definitely needed to disclose this information. It's important to know when people need to know about your illness and when people are better left untold. He shook his head and said he was done talking to me, and I walked away feeling dejected. After leaving the building I turned to go back in to speak more about the incident, but he passed by me and shook his head in disapproval. I knew he wasn't changing his mind.

I was still apprehensive while on campus; I was

afraid people still thought poorly of me and worried about how they would treat me when I ran into them. I returned to my apartment at nights and spent most of my time alone, which was fairly painful. The medication also created melancholy and I didn't know how to cope with the sudden change in emotions from the previous semester. (Usually there are periods of melancholy following episodes, because the manic emotions have diminished or have been completely eliminated and your body is adapting to medication. Medication dims the senses and mollifies emotions and is more potent when you first begin to take it.) The effects and side-effects of the medication eventually subsided after I had taken it for about a month or two, but my body had to adapt to it. I was lonely, depressed, afraid to speak to anyone on campus, and felt I had nowhere to turn, so I only stayed in school for a week that semester and took a medical leave of absence and went home.

After returning home I still had many delusional thoughts. I began organizing the house. I went through every nook and thought of reasons to put objects in certain places. Although it is great to be organized, I was doing this because I still thought external organization would internally create internal organization. I spent most of my time in front of the TV, still well out of touch with reality. I continued to gain weight and I was searching for activities that would help me feel better. I was regaining some sanity but I was changing my ways only in an attempt to conform, rather than thinking through my actions. I constantly watched television and became increasingly passive. I was eating exorbitant amounts of food and not exercising because of my lack of energy. My energy deficiency was a result of overeating, oversleeping, and being over-medicated. I was slipping into a depression.

One of the most difficult things about spending

periods of time at home without an occupation was keeping myself occupied with meaningful activities. I felt completely unproductive and useless, and life itself felt meaningless. During stretches like these, it's important to schedule activities such as reading, exercise, group therapy sessions, volunteering, and maybe even a part-time job once you're capable of holding one. Most important is the discipline to follow through and participate in the activities you've decided on.

I was meeting with a psychiatrist weekly and our sessions were only somewhat helpful. I'd chosen this psychiatrist because his office was a half hour commute against traffic as opposed to an hour of traffic going towards a major city. The doctor located near the major city worked in a renowned psyche hospital and was a specialist for psychotic disorders, but I chose the closer doctor who was a generalist instead. I strongly urge anyone seeking treatment to take the extra time to see the doctor who is most competent in meeting your mental health needs, because it can make all the difference. Specialists are specifically trained and educated to treat patients within their specialty, while generalists are qualified for general neurosis and difficult life issues. If you have a specific illness like schizoaffective disorder a specialist will almost always be better equipped to help you.

The generalist I saw projected the over-professional persona which I had met in the hospital to the point where he wouldn't even shake my hand after sessions. His voice also conveyed objectivity, which I mistook for indifference. It takes courage to confide your innermost feelings to anyone, never mind a stranger, especially when you've been chastised for having any trace of a problem for the vast majority of your life. It is even more difficult to confide in someone who seems indifferent towards you and seems to be merely listening out of professional courtesy. I have found it much easier to connect with people who I have believed actually care about my well-being and at least have a friendly disposition towards me.

I still looked forward to sessions and began talking about everything that had happened during my first episode, but I didn't disclose much personal information. Most of these initial sessions were a recap of the previous six months. We talked about how my delusional thoughts had developed. Another subject I broached was impulsive behaviors during episodes, but we never discussed them in depth. There were some poor decisions I had made which caused people to dislike me but they weren't anything major. I felt an overwhelming feeling of guilt. I thought if my life was going so poorly I must have done something to make it that way. I was extremely hard on myself and thought I was an awful person.

I discovered in later years that the emotions I was feeling weren't connected to my actions. I did make some mistakes while ill and had many argumentative conversations with people and contentious interactions which led to loneliness, but if I was mentally healthy these things wouldn't have happened. I also attribute most of the contentious behaviors and the mistakes I made during episodes mostly to sleeplessness. Going months on end with very little rest was extremely mentally taxing; it made thinking and making decisions difficult. If I was feeling well during therapy I would have been able to dismiss these mistakes as things I had done wrong but weren't a big deal. I was depressed and thought my depression was my fault, when in reality it was a result of my life experiences over the past two years, and my "lameness" from inactivity and being over-medicated.

Sometimes I worried that acquaintances would

ignore me when I ran into them, because I had completely ignored so many people during my episodes. I also feared they would chastise me. I figured everyone would have been talking about all the neurotic and contentious things I had said during episodes.

Therapy continued and I talked about a lot of problems but didn't learn very much. It was more of a venting session than anything else. My doctor used the word *schizophrenia,* but I never actually asked what my diagnosis was because I was afraid to broach the subject.

I was overmedicated and under-stimulated, which made me mentally lethargic and dull, depressed, tired, and hungry; and led to many problems. Although all my psychotic symptoms were completely eliminated with the higher dosages, overmedication gave me new ailments such as a much slower processing speed, a numbness of sensory perception (I felt semi-somnambulant), an exhaustion which made the easiest of tasks mentally and physically draining, and a lack of motivation to do much of anything. My lack of energy and sensory perception was confining. Although my psychotic symptoms were alleviated, the quality and speed of my thinking was immensely diminished and I felt dulled. Overmedication left me depressed and I searched for ways to change my mood to no avail. It's important to note there were other reasons for my depression as well, such as the trauma I had from my experiences, but the mental and physical restrictions were clearly side-effects medications.

Initially everyone experiences strong side-effects, but if a patient is properly medicated the side-effects will subside after two to three months. Being overmedicated is an ailment in itself and eventually caused me to completely stop taking medication altogether, thus resulting in another episode.

My parents had been worried about my behavior over the past couple of years and when I was hospitalized, they informed their friends of my illness. They thought it was for the best. At times, they'd had to make excuses to not hang out with friends because they were visiting a psychiatrist to learn more about me, or were visiting me in the hospital. My parents felt they needed to tell their friends why they had been ditching them. When I discovered that they had informed others of my mental illness, I was livid and stopped talking to them for several days. If you have someone in your family who has a mental illness, I suggest sitting down and asking them if they want others to know. It's important to logically evaluate each situation; sometimes it's necessary for people to know you have an illness and in other situations it's not. My mental health was no one else's business. Although these people were family friends, they certainly didn't need to know about my hospitalization. If there was an incident where something extremely awkward happened, I think it would have been appropriate for people involved in the incident to understand I was mentally ill at the time, but that was not the case. There had been occurrences that were quite awkward—terse conversations, my laughing aloud at my internal monologue—but these could have been easily left in the past without any explanation and without informing people I had a mental illness.

Once people know you have a mental illness they'll sometimes treat you differently. Some become apprehensive that you'll cause them harm. It's unfortunate that when someone does something awful that gets on the news and there are mental health issues involved, people get the impression that they need to be fearful of anyone with a mental illness. Only 4% of all crimes committed have anything to do with mental illness. You are no less safe with someone who has a mental illness than you are with someone who doesn't. There are millions of people with mental health issues who are upstanding citizens just like myself and have never caused anyone any harm.

My parent's friends' knowledge of my mental health issues led to many awkward and embarrassing conversations which were completely unnecessary. Their perception of me was mostly evident in their demeanor and their tone, but I almost felt subhuman while conversing with these people. They would specifically ask how I was currently doing in an overly concerned manner. Although it may have been done in good will, it forced me to think back to a time I was trying to move away from. (It is good to think back and learn about the past, but it was unnecessary to be thinking about it with people I wasn't going to discuss it with.)

I did a lot of self-pitying and thought about how my life would have been had none of this happened. I thought about my old friends graduating that spring and how close they had been; it was painful to think that we weren't friends anymore and I felt quite lonely. I was also estranged from my high school friends who I hadn't hung out with for a long time. I spent most of my time in the basement watching television and wasting away, taking extra Ativan pills hoping I could sleep my way through the day so I could watch sports at night and then go to bed after taking more medication. I only felt good while I was sleeping or eating and almost everything else felt like a chore. Even my conversations were short; I never felt like saying more than a few words to anyone because I was depressed. My mind wasn't working well enough to carry on interesting conversations.

I still hadn't been exercising and I was well overweight, weighing close to 215 lbs. I sometimes went golfing with my Dad to get out of the house, which was some exercise, but not much. That summer I took a Shakespeare course to continue working towards my degree. I thought taking one course would be a good start because I had been out of school for nearly five months. I was afraid of who I'd meet returning to campus, and did actually see some familiar faces. These people were very kind, which surprised me, and it felt good exchanging greetings in passing, but I was still afraid of running into people I knew. I was so accustomed to believing that everyone disliked me that I never actually considered the possibility that they might have dismissed my contentious behaviors, and I decided not to chance reconnecting with old friends. Although I might have been rejected, I could have at least tried to reconnect with my old friends. I would have been no worse off than I was. I completed the Shakespeare course with a passing grade and was happy I did well.

At home, I remembered the adrenaline rush that gambling creates and began playing online poker. My grandfather passed away in my sophomore year of high school and left me some money which I still had saved and I thought I could afford to play a bit. I started playing some of the smaller stakes games but I wasn't very intelligent and I lost a good deal of money. Sometimes I had small victories, which made me think that I would eventually win if I just stuck with it. I blamed most of my losses on bad luck and after several weeks I had lost close to $1000.

That fall I returned to classes to complete my degree. I was living at home and didn't want to return to my previous school. I researched my options and discovered I could attend classes at a school fifteen minutes from home and transfer the credits and still receive a degree from the University. I had three core classes and one general education class remaining. I decided I would spread the course work over two semesters because three core classes were too many to take in one semester. I felt out of place at the new school and was constantly worried about meeting new people. I didn't interact with classmates much at all.

Some guys I used to know called me to play poker and I was lonely and wanted to connect with people my own age. The people I played with knew I needed some friends and used that to lure me to the game. There were no other people in my life at the time and I had nothing else to do so I eagerly attended. They called me "buddy" and "pal" and spoke kindly to me in order to keep me coming to the game. I always had cash because of the inheritance; as long as I was bringing money to the table I was more than welcome to play. They acted as though we were friends but I now realize they only wanted me to feel like I was their friend so they could take my money. Whenever I lost all the cash I had brought with me, they would spot me more money, telling me I could pay them back later so I could continue gambling and losing. The other proof of their using me was that they only called me for poker nights. If we were really friends they would have asked me to hang out at other times, but this never happened. Sometimes I called them just to hang out and they lied about their plans for the night because they wanted to exclude me. I began feeling I had to play cards in order to have any friends and I was losing big.

To my gambling buddies, gambling was a means to obtain money from anyone possible in any way possible. They were proud and eager to lure bad players to the table and take their money. Whenever an inferior player wasn't around, they talked about how awful he was at gambling, greedily anticipating how much they would take from him the next time. At the moment, I was the fish but wasn't willing to admit it to myself and I began losing a lot of money. We played usually one or two nights a week. The buy-in was $100 to start and then you could add as much as you wanted. Some nights I started out winning big and got my chip stack as high as $900, but usually wound up losing all of that money and then some. I initially played some decent poker but I became addicted to the adrenaline rush of gambling. It momentarily pulled me out of the depression I was in and felt like a reprieve. At the start I played rational hands, but it got to a point where I was playing even my worst hands, with the mind set that I just needed a good luck streak to start winning again. I never wanted to believe I could lose and that increased my losses substantially.

I mention this because people who are feeling down, like those with mental health issues who have just had an episode, are more susceptible than others to vices like gambling, drinking, smoking, and anything else that can heighten your emotions. It's important to be careful of how you are medicating your depression and who you are hanging out with. I developed a dangerous addiction to the adrenaline rush of gambling. It was extremely detrimental to my well-being as I continually subjected myself to poor treatment from others in an attempt to alleviate my melancholy and loneliness.

I was with people I had been away from a few years and thought I could trust them, but I was mistaken. I trusted them almost blindly, thinking they would be their previous selves, but they had become avaricious from years of gambling and I paid the price. I was depressed to a point where I talked myself into believing gambling was somehow good for me because I was getting out of the house. There are bad people who will take advantage of you, but the good news is they can only do so if you allow them to. If you know the people you are with aren't treating you right, it's better to move on and look for people who are kind, respectful, and have your best interest in mind. People like that do exist and if you persist you'll find them. This is difficult to do when you are lonely and haven't been invited to hang out with anyone for a while, but sometimes it's better to endure loneliness until you find good people.

My parents knew I was gambling quite a bit and sometimes asked me how I was doing. I usually informed them of my winnings, which were few and far between, and kept quiet about my losses, the way many gamblers do. I wanted them to think I was doing well and knew if they thought otherwise they might intervene and eliminate the one fun event I had in my life. They thought it was good I was getting out and reconnecting with old friends. When I did actually inform them I had lost, I lied about the amount, telling them I lost $50 on an average night when in reality it was usually $400. The reason it was always $400 was because that was the bank's maximum cash withdrawal amount at the time and I couldn't take out any more money. My savings were dwindling. By the semester's end the original $10,000 I began with had decreased to $3000.

I did, however, progress one course closer towards completing my degree. I didn't obtain a passing grade in one class but I did in the other and I was one semester away from my Bachelor's degree. I had no plans for my future and was living moment to moment searching for the smallest scraps of happiness I could find. I realized I had lost a great deal of money, mostly at the live poker game with my supposed friends, and stopped playing there. I felt cheated and robbed but only had my self to blame. It was a difficult situation for me and a learning experience: ultimately it was my decision to attend the game, play poorly, and allow myself to believe that these people were actually my friends. The most difficult part about this was that they had been my friends growing up but had become depraved from gambling and consumed with greed, and I wasn't aware they didn't have my best interest in mind until it was too late. I still had a gambling addiction and continued playing online poker but wasn't losing nearly as much as I did in live games because I played for much lower stakes.

The spring semester arrived and I was excited because I would be completing my degree. One of the remaining courses was a general education course which was fairly easy. I knew at this point I needed something in my life to keep me occupied because my abundance of free time had led to my gambling problems. Thankfully I was taking three classes, which would fill the void. I also obtained a part time job at a local pet store stocking shelves, which helped create some income but mostly got me out of the house and kept me active. There was heavy lifting and the people I worked with weren't very sociable but interacting with customers and managers was beneficial psychologically.

Talking and connecting with others and having laughs felt good. I was able to communicate with people and I knew if I could get along with people at the store, then I could eventually make friends outside of work. I began feeling better and my weight was stabilizing, but I was still exhausted and constantly hungry from overmedication. At that point, I weighed 225 lbs. I checked the scale daily hoping I would lose weight after running 1 mile twice a week but nothing changed. The running at least helped stabilize my weight and the exercise was improving my thinking. I was still fairly depressed and wondered when and how I would be able to make any friends. I lived in a small town and the only people I knew were the people I had grown up with, who obviously weren't my friends. I was afraid to reconnect with the friends I'd made in college, imagining that they thought poorly of me and that their minds were set. I could have reached out to people at my new school but I had convinced myself that I wasn't going to make any friends, rather than staying open to the possibility that I might.

One of the reasons I was lonely at this time was my pessimism. I always believed the worst would happen, and that I would always be depressed. I was convinced before even trying that any attempt at creating any happiness in my life would fail miserably and I talked myself out of attempting to help myself. If I had made an honest effort, I think I would have made some friends and found some happiness.

In early March I was still playing on-line poker and had spent the last penny of the money I had from a $10,000 inheritance. I played a tournament for exactly 1 penny online, hoping I could spark a winning streak and regain everything I had lost. I felt I had a problem and informed my parents of the issue and we deleted my online poker accounts. The pet store job only yielded about $180 per week, so we talked about a way where they could provide me with some extra money, because I was still in school. School was going well and I was on course to pass all my classes and complete my degree; and I was excited because the weather was warming and golf season was approaching. I worked hard at school and at the pet store and was feeling better emotionally. However, although I did my best, I wasn't keeping up at the store because I was usually exhausted. Late that April I was asked to quit my job. With normal energy levels, I would have done well but at the time I was out of shape and lethargic, and just didn't possess the ability to complete the job quickly enough.

Finals arrived that May and I passed them all and graduation was very rewarding.

Although I graduated, I was uncertain of what I wanted to do. Jobs were scarce at the time. I didn't want to work within the vicinity of the university, so I looked for jobs in the opposite direction. In therapy, I hadn't made much progress and was still fairly depressed. I was golfing frequently with my dad; that was all I ever looked forward to.

Chapter 4
Medication - Reasons for Declining and Accepting

That June I went with my family to our time share in Carolina. I began thinking of how much energy I'd had before being medicated and decided to stop taking my medication. I thought the illness was something I could overcome without it; I didn't realize my brain *physically* didn't work the same way it used to. I believed there were issues I could solve that I had not yet addressed which would completely change my psychology and eradicate my illness permanently. I didn't want to be dependent upon medication for the rest of my life and thought I could learn to live without it. I also thought medication was a mark of inadequacy, a sign of weakness, and I felt inferior to others because of my dependency on it. I was too proud to admit that I actually needed help to function properly. I didn't understand the medication was a main component of my recovery and thought I should be able to return to functioning the same way I had before ever developing schizoaffective disorder. I was unaware that there was some sort of physical defect in my brain and attributed my first episode entirely to sleeplessness.

I also didn't understand how schizoaffective disorder develops. To this day doctors are uncertain of the exact cause for its development. With schizophrenia-type illnesses there are always noticeable traces of cognitive impairment earlier in life such as thought blocking, or disorders such as ADD and ADHD. Many people's cognitive impairments never develop into schizophrenia-type illnesses and only one percent of the world's population has schizophrenia. There are theories that state that there is usually some form of trauma in people whose cognitive impairments develop into schizophrenia-type illnesses. There are other theories that posit that schizophrenia-type illnesses are simply neuro-developmental. A neuro-developmental cause means the brain's chemistry and construction has changed as someone has grown older; the brain has developed in a way that causes the schizophrenia-type illness to occur.

I grew up constantly comparing myself to those around me and wanted to be on "the same playing field" as others, not realizing I had a deficiency that gave everyone else an advantage. Medication merely leveled the playing field. I knew other people lived without extra help and I wanted to earn my way through life using the same tools as everyone else. I didn't realize I was short one essential tool and the medication provided me with what I needed. It was no fault of my own that I was missing a fully functioning brain. Now I figure the better off I am, the better off I'll be able to make the people around me—so every advantage I can gain is good for myself and others. This motivates me to take medication because I understand that it helps me function as well as I can, which enables me to help others in my work and in life.

One thing I didn't realize was that I should have just taken every advantage I could get, without concerning myself with comparisons. I now realize it's best for everyone to be as happy as possible; it doesn't matter if I am better or worse than someone else, so long as I am being a good person and I'm happy.

It is smart to take every advantage you can get when attacking mental illness. The more tools the better. Utilizing medication and psychotherapy is a wise decision and an indication that you have the humility and intelligence to be able to use all your available resources.

Swallowing pills takes seconds, and I consider it

a necessary to my mental health, just as food is necessary for maintaining my physical health. People have a "dependency" on food and spend a great deal of time cultivating and consuming it in order to continue living. Going to the pharmacy once a month and picking up a prescription and then taking medication nightly consumes far less time than buying food, preparing it, and then eating it three times per day.

I was also in denial of the many psychological issues that I needed to work out through psychotherapy, and didn't realize doing so would immensely improve the quality of my life. I perceived mental health to be something that was granted at birth; why hadn't this supposed mainstay of human existence been given to me? I felt embarrassed and humiliated that I needed help with something I thought the majority of people were able to do independently: to function normally on a daily basis. People who are uninformed may say that "mental illness" is just an excuse for lack of fortitude or diligence, but this isn't the case at all. There is a great disparity between my functionality while medicated and unmedicated and the illness is no facade for lack of character. I denied my problems because of my embarrassment when in reality there is nothing to be embarrassed or ashamed about. Anyone with the illness comes to understand that it is not lack of character that is causing their mind to malfunction while they are ill. The illness was real and truly changed the way I was able to make decisions, process and create language, even my ability to sleep.

A diagnosis can be extremely beneficial but also detrimental. When I was initially diagnosed, I was afraid to even mention the name of the illness I had because I didn't understand what the diagnosis meant. I attached a stigma to the words "schizoaffective disorder" and "schizophrenia," fearful that there must be something wrong with my personality. I thought having schizoaffective disorder was unnatural, that there was something weird about me because I was diagnosed with it. There were oddities in my personality at the time from having experienced psychosis and other psychological trauma, but I later eliminated most of these through talk therapy. When first told my diagnosis, I thought that having schizoaffective disorder meant I would be stuck in the state of being I was in, the same way someone with a physical handicap is. I thought it was incurable and didn't have much hope I would ever overcome it.

I later came to understand the meaning of the diagnosis and was more comfortable with accepting that I had an illness, just as someone can have something like a cold. The only difference between my mind and others is that my functionality is impaired while unmedicated and sometimes even while medicated. I have experienced symptoms that are fairly odd, such as referential thinking, paranoia, and auditory hallucinations. Observing the effect of these symptoms on my behavior from a bystander's point of view might lead you to believe that people with mental health issues are odd, but these symptoms brought on by the illness are completely unrelated to my personality and my character. When people witness someone acting in an unusual way, they may consider the person's behavior "weird." They may associate the perceived "weirdness" with perversion. But having a mental illness certainly is not an indication of perversion; it simply means your mind's functionality is different than that of other people's.

I had imagined that having mental illness put me in an exclusive minority, but about **half the population** seeks mental health assistance for some sort of issue(s).

The detriment of being given a diagnosis is that

the patient can use it as an excuse for making mistakes and having a lower quality of life. For a while I used my diagnosis as an excuse and didn't do much to help myself. Believing and accepting that I had an incurable problem was detrimental for me. If I had never changed my perception of my illness and learned to see it as something that was curable, I never would have overcome it. I think some people just accept the illness and don't work to figure out which parts of the illness they can eliminate and which they have to accept. I've found I've been able to eliminate most of the detriments of the illness through medication, problem solving, and therapy, and by creating strategies to negotiate symptoms like referential thinking and other ailments.

I used to believe that most psychological issues were gripes or complaints that people needed to solve on their own; I didn't realize their complexity or the importance of working through them. Talking about and working through a problem with the help of a trusted advisor is far more intelligent than allowing a problem to exist. If I can't solve a problem by thinking it through, I know the smart thing to do is to ask someone else's opinion, and many times the person I go to with questions is my psychotherapist. That is the way psychotherapy works. Everyone deserves to have someone they can talk to about life's questions.

Most successful people benefit from some form of outside help even while they are helping themselves. Intellectuals, doctors, scientists, and researchers are usually well-educated but none of them would have obtained their education if other people were not willing to share their knowledge. Information gained from research is also a form of help, because the knowledge was acquired from someone else's work. The world goes round because people are willing to help each other and work together. Even when the most independent of people are helping themselves they often utilize resources someone else has created.

With mental illness, getting help comes in the form of taking medication and using your psychotherapist as a resource. I meet people daily who don't have anything physically wrong with their brains but still have delusional thoughts and psychological imperfections which impede their functionality. These hindrances did not result from episodes but simply from negative experiences in their lives. I believe mental health check-ups should be just as regular as physicals because of the benefits of psychotherapy. Many people are already benefiting from medication but *everyone* can benefit from psychotherapy.

When I stopped taking the medication all my emotional detriments were instantly alleviated. My thinking pace drastically improved while my sensory perceptions returned to full functionality. It felt as though I had stepped out of slow motion back into the regular pace of life. I was happier and was beginning to feel the adrenaline of mania I had previously felt; my energy levels increased substantially. This led me to believe I had made the right decision. During our vacation-stay at the time share, I went to the gym daily and ran at least one mile every day and lifted weights too. I was happy because I felt I could function again and my depression lifted.

After medicating for an extended period, patients usually retain the medication's effect for approximately one to two months after the date they stopped taking it. That is because the medication is still in the patient's body; the system requires time to filter it out. Once I stopped taking the medication the side-effects were gone but the benefits of being medicated were still present for the first month or so.

I had never explored the option of reducing my medication with my psychiatrist; doing so would have been very beneficial. Some doctors may overmedicate to eliminate symptoms completely, and then cut back over time to minimize side-effects, because they feel the symptoms of the mental illness can be far more dangerous than those of the side-effects. Eliminating the illness takes priority. But I found I was better off having far less medication; dealing with the symptoms of schizoaffective disorder first hand was easier than being over-medicated. Being over-medicated was an ailment in itself for me, which led to depression and influenced me to stop taking the medication altogether resulting in another episode.

Being over-medicated left me emotionally dead, extremely lethargic physically and mentally, feeling incapable of doing much of anything, unmotivated to do anything, and extremely depressed. I didn't have any of the things I wanted out of life. Over-medication left me feeling suicidal at times. I was well overweight; I didn't have a job, friends, a girlfriend, or any meaningful activities to participate in. Comparing my life during my episodes to my life while over-medicated, I decided that my life during my episodes was better than the life I was living while being over-medicated. That's the reason I stopped taking medication all together.

As this second episode developed, my parents frequently requested that I return to taking the medication but I adamantly and vehemently rejected the idea. I could tell my health was slowly diminishing without it, but my only perception of being medicated was being over-medicated; it never occurred to me that less medication could be the key.

As my health deteriorated during this second episode I had a lot of angry outbursts. These outbursts were the result of frustration, the feeling there was no possible way for me to get the things I wanted out of life. I felt stuck between the only two options available to me, both horrible: one, being over-medicated—which I knew didn't work, and the other, going without medication, which was leading to psychosis. I felt I'd never get out of this situation and I'd never have the things I wanted out of life.

I think that among the most essential things any person could want are friendship and love. That is what I desired most during my episodes and after. I frequently thought about how I could make friends or—somehow—have a relationship. Sherwood Anderson wrote a great story called "Seeds" where he states that the root of psychological problems is a person's feeling that he or she is going to be alone. That was my greatest and constant fear. My loneliness and fear of being alone forever really shook me and created a lot of negative emotions during the development and experience of both my episodes, and that fear continued for several years following my second episode.

The doctor I am currently seeing prescribed a lower level of medication, which left me with symptoms of schizoaffective disorder for several years but allowed me to retain functionality, energy, and processing ability. I eventually made friends and obtained the things I wanted out of life. The lower dose of 2 mg Risperidone (as opposed to the cocktail of high dosages of other drugs I had been taking) made all the difference. I was able to live a much better life than I had than when I was over-medicated.

I was still somewhat paranoid, a bit neurotic, socially dysfunctional, and had symptoms of referential thinking. I began work in talk therapy and over the years I discovered many of the symptoms I was experiencing stemmed from traumatic experiences that I needed to address, and I found alleviation from addressing these issues. Part of the reason I was able to address these issues was being forced to face them on a daily basis. I'm currently a high functioning individual; people have no idea that I have schizoaffective disorder.

If someone had approached me during the development of this second episode to inform me that if I took a lower dose of medication the quality of my life could be different, I definitely would have considered it. I didn't realize it was an option. After two months of taking only 2 mg risperidone following my second episode, I still had energy to exercise, which is vital to living a healthy life style. I obtained a job within a year, I made some friends after about a year and a half, and, most importantly, I was able to think and make decisions and didn't feel lethargic. I still had psychotic symptoms and many fears, but as I worked through these in talk therapy, my mental functionality improved and I made more friends and began getting what I wanted out of life. My current doctor, who I started seeing after my second episode, had difficulty getting me to take the lower dose of medication, but I eventually decided to try it. The lower dosage allowed me to live a much better life than when I was overmedicated, even though I still had many schizoaffective symptoms.

Chapter 5
My Second Episode

After returning home from vacation I started believing in some of the same delusions I had believed in during my first episode. I wanted to save the world and I believed anyone could do anything if they set their mind to it, so I decided I would become a professional golfer who would make millions of dollars and donate to those in need. As in my first episode, I believed dreams were never to be spoken of, or they would fade away and never become accomplished. My actions were directly influenced by the belief I could save the world, but no one else had any idea what I was thinking.

I began taking many trips to the golf course and practicing regularly. I believed physical conditioning was essential to my golf game (which it is), and I was losing four pounds a week. I was excited that I was losing weight because restoring my physical health was physically and emotionally energizing. I exercised regularly and began a strict diet. The exercise made me happier, as did all the benefits which exercise produces. I was more flexible, felt healthier, and moved with greater ease. Exercise also facilitates thinking and my thinking was much clearer than it had been while I was medicated. These improvements strengthened my belief that ceasing my medication was the right decision.

My diet consisted of the recommended daily quantities on the USDA food guide pyramid. I also asked my mom if she would buy all organic food, but she informed me the prices were high and she would buy what she could. This was a good compromise and made me feel better because I was attempting to eat organic. I knew organic food wasn't entirely affordable, and was also pacified by thinking if the entire world were to suddenly convert to all organic food there would be food shortages and famine.

I felt revitalized. My parents noticed all the positives of my having stopped my medication, but they still insisted I continue going to psychotherapy and taking medication. I had noticed too many benefits from being unmedicated and had already decided that I wouldn't be returning to the previous misery I had experienced, which I believed resulted from medication. I readily agreed to attend psychotherapy sessions, stating that, as long as I didn't have to take any medication, this would be perfectly acceptable. They were still apprehensive about my not taking it but hadn't noticed any of my symptoms returning yet, and for that reason they were less rigid about allowing me not to take it. In psychotherapy, I was asked if I was taking my medication and informed my psychiatrist I had stopped, but would still be attending talk therapy sessions. He informed me this could be dangerous and asked I take it, so I began lying about having taken medication. Whenever he asked, I informed him I was medicated. He never broached the idea of taking lower doses of medication rather than going back to the full amounts originally prescribed.

During the summer, I continued to lose weight. I was improving my golf game and believed I could join the PGA tour after one summer of practice; I was convinced I was an agent of divinity again. This is another story I look back on and find humor in. I'm currently a 14 handicap and won't be qualifying for the play-in to any PGA event, but it's funny to think I once believed I was bound for the tour.

I thought it was my parents' job to provide for me while I pursued this goal and assumed that they realized it was their duty to help me become a professional golfer. This led to some strife. After a while I realized I needed to help around the house and did so willingly. I wondered how anyone could have diverted me from pursuing my goal of saving the world, and I returned to believing in all my first episode delusions while also creating new ones.

I again adopted the belief that everything external is reflected internally, so I reorganized the clutter that my room had become. There are many behaviors during episodes that can be good in theory but are done for the wrong reasons. I also cleaned the entirety of my bathroom, from ceiling to floor, thinking that would purify it, which would improve my thinking.

I slept in the basement in a sleeping bag on the floor because I believed my room was still dirty and couldn't be slept in. I slept on the floor because I thought I would be sleeping "6 feet under" if I were on the couch, in a ghostly world where spirits would haunt me. After a few weeks of sleeping on the basement floor I cleaned my room. I cleaned my ceiling three different ways, washed the walls, and hired a professional carpet cleaner to steam my rug. Twice. I then cleaned the interior of my car, which took me at least six hours.

My temper was returning and I was showing signs of aggravation while speaking to my parents. Some of our conversations were very cordial while others were contentious; I was uncertain whether or not they were on my side again. I would yell at my mom during conversations about righteousness and propriety and apologize afterwards, feeling awful about what I had said to her. This persisted throughout the episode and got worse with time.

It was August and I weighed about 185 lbs. I was golfing mostly with my Dad or alone because most of my old friends knew something was awry but weren't able to pinpoint it, and didn't want to hang out with me because of it. I had an irascible temper. While attempting to plan a golf outing with one friend, I got frustrated and hung up the phone and cussed loudly after hanging up. This was on a driving range at a private course. Many heads were turned but I didn't think much of it at the time. My temper was uncontrollable in situations where I was upset and the anger would come out verbally. The anger built up and I attempted holding it in but —just as a person standing straight up can't resist falling forward if someone shoves them from behind— I couldn't help but release the anger. The words slipped out and I knew immediately after it happened that I'd made a mistake, but it was too late. That was also the type of anger I directed at my mom.

While running at night I was checking the street lights again for portents, just as I had during the first episode. My communication ability was still intact and I was making sense while talking. My parents were noticing signs of deteriorating health and intermittently asked me if I was feeling all right. My response was always that I was feeling well. They explained their logic and would show me examples of how my actions were similar to those of my first episode, but I talked them out of their concerns and diverted the conversation to different subjects. I knew I was repeating behaviors from my previous episode but was in partial denial that my health was headed in the same direction. I found reasons why these same behaviors were somehow different and continued carrying them out. I wanted to believe I could exist without the medication because my only conception of being medicated was that of being *over*medicated.

I was unable to see how I was becoming increasingly more delusional, just as I had during the first episode. Something the two episodes had in common is that they developed over time. The first one took about two years to fully develop and then lasted for six to eight months, but the second episode became full fledged after about three months. That is close to the amount of time it takes to use up all the medication in the system. For some people, each episode is physically damaging to the brain, and as more episodes occur, mental health deteriorates further and it becomes increasingly more difficult to return to healthy states of being after each episode.

Talk therapy sessions with my psychiatrist were at a standstill and I was becoming very terse. He asked me questions which I thought were personal and invasive. Many questions psychiatrists ask are personal but they are intended to help patients in full confidentiality. This was something I didn't understand. I thought it was painful and detrimental for me to answer his questions. I struggled through sessions thinking if I did answer any questions I would be doing myself a disservice. I thought it was pointless to revisit past memories which were painful, not realizing that there were issues from these occurrences still residing in my psyche that needed to be rooted out. I didn't understand that finding the reasons for my trauma and problems and creating solutions would be beneficial for my mental health and would immensely improve my well-being.

At the end of August I began feeling extremely unstable. I felt an overwhelming angst and uneasiness which was difficult to bear. I was still highly energetic and had only been sleeping four or five hours a night after working out sometimes twice a day or golfing. I should have been exhausted enough to sleep at least eight to ten hours. The adrenaline-feeling was becoming stronger and was developing into mania and I was becoming increasingly addicted to it again. I sat on the back porch at night stargazing, confused about my situation.

I believed things happen for a reason and thought I must have done something wrong in order for my life to unravel the way it had the past several years. I told myself "You deserve what you get," and attributed my hardships from mental illness to the accumulation of wrong I had done throughout my life. I thought through my entire life and only recalled bad experiences, not realizing that many kids make the same mistakes I did. I felt my life was a failure up to this point.

I thought the best thing I could do to eliminate all the psychosis, bipolarity, and sleeplessness would be to apologize to everyone for everything wrong I had ever done or thought I had ever done. I believed that by doing so I would start a global chain where everyone would ask forgiveness for the wrongs they had done. People were confused when I apologized to them because they couldn't think of anything I had actually done wrong and thought it was strange I was apologizing for things I either didn't do or that were fairly innocuous. Some people even asked if I was on the 12-step program, but I wasn't.

I still trained regularly for golf and was running as much as 5 to 6 miles three times a week in order to condition my body. I had a warm up and stretching routine which I thought was mandatory and worried that my golf game would flounder if I didn't implement this routine correctly before playing. I also made certain that my morning routine was precisely the way I thought it should be, starting over if I missed any step. I was spending time in reverie pacing back and forth in a fervor. (Even today I still pace and my family has come to accept it, but it's much different than it was during episodes.)

That September I came up with some ideas I thought would help improve the world and secure humanity's survival. One of them was creating a pipeline leading from the warmer climates to the North and South Poles which would pump water back to the poles. Upon reaching the poles the water would then freeze, resulting in a decrease in global temperatures and water levels. I thought if a vacuum was created on one end it would propel the water through the pipeline. Another thought of mine was that, by moving land from the Kenyan mountains into northwest Africa, humanity could eventually build a mountain range there. The Sahara Desert would become fertile because of the volume of fresh water that would accumulate. I thought there would be a new place for people to inhabit; overpopulated countries could send people to live in this new region. I was excited about these ideas and contacted an old professor to inform him of them. I really thought my ideas were going to work. We spoke once and he was kind but we didn't speak again. I didn't think he was going to act on my ideas, which was true.

I then proceeded to contact my uncle who worked for the government. He told me he thought they were good ideas and he would let someone know. He realized I wasn't feeling well; he knew about my mental illness and acted as though he was taking me seriously in order to pacify me. He then proceeded to inform my parents of our conversation and they attempted to get me back on the medication. During this time, I was unaware that they knew about my ideas. Eventually I began to doubt that they were on my side again, because they wanted me to revert to a practice which had previously failed miserably for me and I wasn't willing to do that. I thought the medication was the only reason I had been depressed, not realizing that I had gone through some extremely adverse experiences and the issues from these experiences were affecting me subconsciously and damaging my psyche. These issues were the main reason I had so much anger during my second episode.

That September I visited some friends for a party

at their apartment and had difficulty getting along with them. We talked about things they liked and I blatantly disagreed about some television commercial, which created tension. We got in an argument over the morality of football. I wound up getting in another argument later, yelling at the top of my lungs in a disagreement over a trivial matter; and then I nearly got into a fist fight with a third person. I thought it was my responsibility to change people for their own well-being. Throughout this episode there was a great deal of strife when I disagreed with someone over even the slightest of differences. After that night people hung out with me very infrequently.

I was still golfing as frequently as possible. I played in the cold weather through October and into November until it snowed. I was still in good physical condition and in October I ran a 5k in twenty minutes and nine seconds. My temper was becoming increasingly more uncontrollable and I was yelling more frequently than ever. Even when my windows and doors were shut, someone would be able to hear me from 50 yards across the street.

I was beginning to recycle more items. I looked for any scraps of cardboard, paper, plastic, and metal that were out of use and could be taken away. Many of the items I took needed to be gotten rid of, such as broken-down exercising machinery and antiquated computer monitors in our basement, so my parents partially viewed what I was doing as a big help but also recognized it as one of my symptoms from my first episode. I actually threw away other items that I still needed, like the cardboard backing to my bureau.

I thought I needed to conserve electricity as much as possible. I kept as few lights on as possible, dimming them to the lowest setting. I thought that would reduce my carbon foot print, which in turn would prevent ozone depletion and save the world. (Ironically, more electricity is used when the lights are on the dimmers and less when they're not being dimmed, but I was unaware of this.) I often walked around the house at night in the dark and my eyes began to adjust. But this was fairly creepy to the rest of my family. I was still losing weight. When we dined out for my birthday, the waiter asked if I was 18 when I was really 23.

I began believing magic was real and I was actually waiting for a letter to inform me when my magical training would begin. In fourth grade a rock had somehow become imbedded in my neck and we never were able to determine how this happened. The rock probably got lodged under my skin when I fell down somewhere outside. However, I thought it was one of the magical occurrences which, in the Harry Potter series, are said to happen to young wizards and witches before they are sent their letter from Hogwarts, which informs them they have magical power and means they have the ability to become a witch or wizard. I was excited to become a wizard and was anticipating the arrival of my letter. (Yes, it's all right—you can laugh. I still laugh about it myself.)

I wasn't making any progress in psychotherapy because I was unwilling to speak to my psychiatrist anymore. I was afraid of the questions he would ask me and still didn't want to broach painful subjects. We got to a point late that October where he informed me he wouldn't be able to help me if I was unwilling to talk and would have to stop accepting me as a patient altogether because of my lack of progress. Any professional should have been able to recognize my reticence as a symptom; he should have never terminated me as a patient. To this day I'm uncertain why he made that decision. He left me his phone number and told me that if I needed anything I could always call.

As time went on my delusions increased, as did the the extent to which I carried out my delusions.

It was the Wednesday before Thanksgiving. A bunch of my parents' friends were coming over on Thanksgiving for dessert. I prepared the house fever-ishly. I thought if I was going to do anything it had to be absolutely perfect, otherwise I wasn't going to do it at all. I went into the kitchen to clean the chairs and asked my sister to move so I could vacuum but she didn't feel like it. She said I could come back later and—instead of moving for a few seconds—she stayed. Although I did have a reason to be upset with her, because I had been cleaning the house all day, I didn't need to yell. I flipped out. My irascible temper took control and I cursed at her. My mom tried to intervene and I yelled at her too, and I went off in a storm. I decided to go to the base-ment where I could sit alone and watch TV until I went out later that night, but my Dad came downstairs to yell at me. He addressed me with a stern tone, as if he was going to tell me what to do and take control of the situa-tion. I nearly fought him. He pointed a finger at me and tried telling me what I could and could not do and I started yelling at him. I was sitting on the couch when this began and he was across the room. After he start-ed yelling at me, I rose and walked over and stood straight up to him, to inform him I wasn't going to be controlled. I then informed him he had no say in what my actions would be; I was not going to yield to his at-tempts at intimidating me. He actually *was* attempting to intimidate me as he had done when I was younger, and I wasn't going to stand for it. He thought that the "child" should listen to the "parent," and if not he should be coerced into listening out of fear.

Feeling compelled to do something out of fear felt very arresting and imprisoning and bogged me down. During my childhood, I was made to fear wrong-doing and fear my Dad while he was yelling. He wanted to be the only authority and there was no talking back whatsoever. His yelling created problems for me throughout my childhood, when I was unable to stand up for myself for fear of being yelled at. That childhood experience made me fearful of being intimidated into doing anything. Already fairly paranoid from schizoaffective disorder, I didn't want to be coerced into doing anything, and this interaction put me over the edge. In the past I had rarely—if ever—stood up to him, but this time I did. He was scared and informed me he was going to call the police and have them arrest me. I told him he couldn't do that.

I compromised and said I would call my psychiatrist, which I did. After talking to him for a bit, I apologized to my family for yelling and ignored the fact that my dad did attempt to intimidate me into listening to him. I then went out to the bar to meet up with friends for our annual Thanksgiving get-together. That night was rather awkward and I had many disjointed conversations. Some people were avoiding me because they could tell something was wrong, but I didn't notice it much at the time. Others spoke to me briefly and then searched for ways out of the conversation.

The next night I went to my 5-year high school reunion and it was no different. I nearly fought a friend from high school because he was trying to convince almost every attractive girl he saw to go home with him.

Later that night, after our time at the bar, I was walking with a friend to an apartment. As we passed Prospect Street I said, "This is Prospect Street, you know." I was inferring that he was a prospect for righteous living and was on the right path. I thought I was on the spiritually correct path myself and it was my responsibility to get everyone else going in the same direction— but could only throw out hints because each person needed to decide for himself. He looked at me and said "Oh, okay," uncertain of how to react because he had no idea what I was thinking. I thought I was creating a metaphor that he would pick up on and that would change his life. I was thinking metaphorically again, slowly losing my ability to see how many occurrences in life are completely unrelated to each other.

We arrived at the apartment and I almost got in another fight with the guy who had been womanizing at the bar. He had his feet up on the refrigerator which was close to the couch and I yelled at him about not having any respect. I told him he should take his feet down.

Later that night, I left with some friends, but pulled over two or three times on the way home to think about whether I needed to go back to get another one of my friends. with us. I asked my friends if I should go back for him when we were already half way home. I drove about a tenth of a mile further and asked the same question, not once but twice. They asked me what I was doing and told me I needed to keep driving; I eventually got us home.

Three weeks passed and my intelligibility of speech was decreasing and other symptoms were getting worse. I wasn't talking with my dad but was getting along with my mom and she attempted to talk to me about how I might need to go to the hospital. The instant they mentioned the hospital I became afraid; I thought back to how I had "barely escaped my last hospitalization." I was afraid I could be kept there indefinitely and declined to go. I felt lucky I was un-hospitalized; because of the stigma created by popular culture, I thought of psychiatric hospitals as horrible places where patients are tortured. I was determined to do everything possible to avoid going there. I changed my behavior and tried to lay low, to avoid being sent there.

Despite my "good behavior," signs of my illness were obvious and my parents persisted in asking me to check in. I always declined, hoping they would notice improvements in my behavior and decide I didn't need to go.

My friends were hosting a Christmas party on December 17th and I was excited to hang out with people again. I had spent most of the past eight months in solitude and was always happy when I could get out and socialize. The main reason I was so isolated was my mercurial personality, edginess, and inability to have positive social interactions. I arrived at the party determined not to drink because I knew I would have issues if I did. Their apartment was located in a major city, in a decent neighborhood surrounded by some tougher neighborhoods. The night started out pleasantly but went downhill as people became more intoxicated. Earlier in the evening I said to a friend's younger brother, "Just listen to me," partly kidding. Later that evening I thought everything he was doing was a direct result of my telling him to listen. He started a fight with another friend of ours, strangling him maliciously for about fifteen seconds until four or five other guys were able to pull him off. Later that evening he head-butted a girl and everyone was up in arms.

All of this happened after I had decided to try someone else's drink, taking just one sip of alcohol. After the sip, I felt completely disoriented. I attributed my state of mind to drunkenness, but it was actually due to my mental illness. I thought the alcohol turned a switch in my mind, which from then on would not stay inside my head; it had become the impetus for everyone's actions in the real world. I thought everything happening around me was set in motion by my psyche and my conscious thoughts. I thought the strange things happening at the party were caused by my drinking the alcohol (although I had nothing to do with the commotion and wasn't the cause of any of it). It was a ridiculously miserable night; many things happened that I have never seen happen before.

I had completely lost any trust I had in my own decision-making ability; I thought I needed to do things people around me were doing. As had happened in my earlier episode, I began to think I saw people hinting at things I should do. If people looked in a certain direction, I thought they were hinting at me to go that way, so I did, and I proceeded to do this for some period of time.

I thought I needed to recreate the incident where my friend's brother strangled our other friend, in order to reverse the effect of the world being a product of my mind and stop the madness of the night. So I put my hands around the neck of the person who had been strangled earlier, as if I too were strangling him, but without applying any pressure.

Later in the night someone tried hooking up with a girl who was almost completely passed out. Someone stopped him, but at this point I decided I needed to leave, because it was my mind's having flipped inside out that was causing all of this. All of the bad things happening that night were things I have never done myself, but somehow, I still believed the chaos in my own mind was generating all the negative occurrences.

I snuck out the door around 1:00 am and caught a taxi at a nearby station and asked the cabby if he could drive me home. (I thought my leaving would help restore order throughout the world.) My home was an hour away and the cabby was uncertain of where I wanted to go. I was unintelligible and he asked me for my phone so he could call home and ask where I lived. A couple times I asked him to just drop me off, telling him I would make my way to my sister's apartment (which was in a completely different section of the city). We continued driving and I was afraid if I got out before arriving at the correct destination the world would end. He spoke to my dad and drove me to a local branch of my dad's work where I would be picked up and taken care of. On the way, I began laughing hysterically and pissed myself in the cab. When the cab stopped, I was afraid to put my foot on the ground because I thought the world would end. I was encouraged and told it would be all right and finally agreed to get out of the cab. I waited in the security room of the local branch and was eventually drugged and driven by ambulance to a psychiatric hospital.

The hospital campus was built at least 100 years ago. Most of the buildings were brick with paved walk-ways and well-landscaped areas. There were some artificial ponds and many trees and plants. The buildings were well-lit and were painted bright colors and had bright tiles. The unit I stayed at consisted of two main hallways with patient rooms branching off, as well as a dining area, recreation room, arts room, and nurse's station. In the common areas, there were paintings of landscapes and posters with positive messages such as "Be the change you wish to see". The rooms had high ceilings and many windows and were usually furnished with two beds, two bureaus, two stand-in closets, and a desk, all made of lightly stained wood.

During my first few days of hospitalization I was exhausted and would have slept the majority of the time had the staff not awoken me and requested I participate in the daily activities. I was given sleeping medication and for the first time in three months I was able to sleep for more than four hours, which improved my well-being. At this time, I weighed about 150 lbs and the staff encouraged me to eat as much as possible in order to

regain the missing weight. I wore hospital clo'
first night but my family eventually brought me ou~.
things to wear and it was comforting having my own
clothing. After breakfast, I would check in with a staff
member and have my vitals taken, which informed the
staff how my system was reacting to medication and
gave some indication of how I felt physically. While my
vitals were being taken, I strove to be as calm as possible, believing that my calmness was essential to
keeping everyone on the unit calm. I still thought my
own thoughts and actions had an affect on everyone
else's mind, so I relaxed myself to a point where my vitals were always excellent. Outside of these readings I
was still manic, as the staff probably knew through ob-
servation.

As did the other patients, I then checked in with
a staff member and informed them how I was doing,
what was bothering me, and some of the issues on my
mind. After this there was a morning talk therapy group
where we discussed mental health issues and shared
our experiences, thoughts, and feelings with the group
and sometimes requested feedback about how to handle situations. Lunch followed, and after that we had an
afternoon group which taught us different therapeutic
and coping strategies for times when we were feeling
particularly stressed. There was also art therapy, which
was free-time for creativity, supervised gym and recreation room trips, and walks around the campus for
which passes were mandatory.

During my first couple of nights I roomed with
someone who was a victim of child militancy. He had
fought and killed people from age twelve forward in
South American wars which had been traumatizing for
him. He was found at the top of a bridge before being
hospitalized. He was a nice person but it was evident
he was traumatized. My first night sleeping in the room

with him, I had awful nightmares which were related to his story. This led me to believe I was telepathic and actually able to listen to someone else's thoughts. I experienced awful nightmares, but they were mostly due to an initial side-effect of Trazodone. I was switched to Seraquel after the staff was informed I was having nightmares.

I made some friends. Many people were experiencing similar symptoms and I was excited to be able to interact with others who were similar to me. This was the first time in months that I was warmly accepted into a group where my opinion was valued and people were genuinely interested in me. Whenever I was asked how my hospitalization was going, I informed the staff that it was going well. Some of them thought I was being smart, but there were many parts of the experience I genuinely enjoyed. I was regaining weight which had been lost over the past four months, I was medicated and my thinking was improving, I was obtaining a full-night's rest again which was also very helpful, and I was close to people and socializing. I had been spending almost all of my time alone, dating as far back as my first hospitalization, so interacting with others was very enjoyable.

While hospitalized I still believed I was an agent of divinity who needed to be successful during my hospitalization in order to save the world. I made friends with an aristocrat who had insider's information on world affairs, and she pulled me aside one night to inform me of some grave news. She was unable to see any countries in Eastern Europe on her live internet maps and told me she thought Israel had been nuked and Europe was enveloped in nuclear fallout. This hospitalization was during the North Korean standoff with the nuclear artillery, so it seemed plausible to me at the time that something may have happened. She told me

Iran had nuked Israel, and she said she was unable to contact the president of her country, which meant the situation was dire because, as she had informed me, she was always able to contact him.

This information led me to believe her and as a result, I befriended a Chinese pianist who had immigrated to the US who was also on the unit. I knew China was allied with North Korea and thought the friendship of someone of American and Chinese descent would help the respective governments make peace because of the telegraphic network I thought I was a part of. I continued talking and hanging out with the aristocrat and told her I wanted to become a writer. She spoke to me of her belief that messiahs would rise up and save the world; she talked about Nobel laureates and mentioned that she thought I would become one. This perpetuated my belief that I needed to become a writer and do everything correctly in order to save the world.

I began organizing my few possessions, still believing that external organization leads to internal organization. I was happy to wake up and be with friends every morning and hung out with the aristocrat daily. I met a Harvard English professor and we spoke about religion. I began praying again before meals, which was something I had previously done on my own but hadn't been doing recently. I studied religion during my hospitalization and at the time it was pacifying. Some people with emotional disorders dislike religion, citing it as an impetus for delusional behavior, but I found it useful at the time. I am currently agnostic but still use the best of what I've gleaned from having studied religion.

I met someone claiming to be a philosopher who taught classes and we spoke about Existentialism; I thought I needed to demonstrate some of what I knew. I thought I needed to to teach him. I created clues and hinted at my thoughts because I thought he needed to figure them out in order to earn the knowledge by his own merit. In one such instance I opened the door as wide as possible without it touching the backstop in order to create as much space as possible in the room; I thought doing so would create space within my own mind and everyone else's. I believed that physical objects should be separated as much as possible because if they were touching, it would muddle a person's ability to properly separate them mentally.

In the hospital, there were many people with short tempers who I overheard yelling at family members at the top of their lungs. There were others who were quiet and kept mostly to themselves. I met one woman who thought she was clairvoyant and to this day I am uncertain whether there is such a thing as clairvoyance. It's something I have never experienced myself, but I can't entirely rule it out. She told me she had seen the ghosts of a massacre on a beach one day, and later learned there was a colonial massacre in the same location where she had seen these ghosts. She had difficulty being at the hospital because of all the spirits there. I entertained her inquiries, relatively uncertain of how to react. I was as kind as possible, and I made friends. I think the best rule for behavior in a hospital is to understand that other people have ailments and you need to be as respectful as possible whenever they convey information; these people genuinely believe in their thoughts and will be insulted if you don't listen respectfully. If you are hospital staff, patients may be disinclined to talk to you if you don't take them seriously.

This woman was very personable and I enjoyed talking to her. She was a beautiful woman in her early forties and was married with children. She also believed that she had been reincarnated from a previous life.

There were other people in her life who she stated were also reincarnated, and she told me of one conversation in particular where some dude informed her he had lived with her in one of their past lives and she believed him. She thought she needed to stay in contact with this dude because of the affinity of their having experienced past lives together. I personally have no belief in reincarnation and am inclined to think this was a ruse by the dude to be closer to her. I mention this because being mentally ill as a woman is far more dangerous than as a man; if you know women who aren't feeling well it's especially important to look out for them.

I was fairly positive and avoided using any words with negative denotations, such as "No," or "Don't." There was another patient who was quite distraught who I had difficulty coping with. She thought I was being positive to annoy her because she was morbidly depressed and had trouble being positive. It was merely the way I was and I didn't mean anything by it—but I usually avoided her because I knew my positivity was a problem.

Reading the body language of my fellow patients helped me to realize when they might act out or simply want to be alone. Just about every patient in the unit was unapproachable at one time or another. There were many instances where people were crying and were extremely upset, and they expressed their sorrow periodically throughout the day. Older patients were usually better at coping with ailments than younger ones. I usually tried to avoid people during those times. I tried to maintain a positive mind set. One of the difficulties of being in a psychiatric unit was enduring the episodic behavior of other patients. During my first hospitalization, the other patients were in much better health than in this unit, so interacting with them was fairly easy, because they were more mentally composed.

Sometimes hospitalization can be triggering and psychotic behavior can be contagious for someone with mental illness. I felt an extreme foreboding and was somewhat paranoid as an in-patient, because it was such a precarious place where seemingly anything could happen. Sometimes people would act out uncontrollably, and there were several instances during my nine days being hospitalized when a girl ran down the halls impulsively until she was restrained by the staff. There were other people who had irascible tempers (like I did) who would yell with truculent anger over the phone. The stress of the other patients began wearing on me. My positivity was still intact but was difficult to maintain because people were usually talking about their ailments or were extremely upset over past experiences.

Most people who are in-patients have experienced trauma and share their experiences during group sessions. Interacting with people who have similar ailments was helpful and educational. One of the best takeaways from group therapy in the hospital was learning there are many people who have mental illnesses and seek help regularly for them. By attending group therapy, I learned that my issues were quite common. Even in my everyday life, when I talked to people about my mental illness, they usually respond by sharing some ailment they are dealing with, whether it be depression, anxiety, trauma, or any number of things. I've come to learn that the majority of people have some sort of adversity in their lives, even if they aren't mentally ill.

At the beginning of each group everyone checks in and then volunteers mental health topics they would like to discuss. The group listens to their questions and answers as well as possible. Many people have mutual problems. Thinking about other people's experiences is helpful because I'm able to apply the lessons they've learned to my own life.

Group therapy can also be taxing if it is constant; towards the end of my hospitalization I volunteered less information, simply because I felt it was becoming increasingly more difficult to bear emotionally. I still participated and answered others' questions as best I could. Many people had reason to be distressed, and a main component of improving mental health is talking with others about ailments.

At nights, I usually played chess with a friend who was a text book writer and I enjoyed our literary conversations.

The staff were friendly and helpful and created a warm environment and they genuinely cared for the well-being of the patients. Patients talked and interacted with staff daily, most of whom had a genuine interest in helping their patients. They were interesting people and we enjoyed jovial conversations about everyday subjects.

The doctor, however, approached our conversations with the same indifference shown by my previous two doctors; he made me nervous about my hospitalization. He asked me questions which I felt more inclined to answer, but I didn't trust him either. I was worried I would be kept indefinitely as some people are in movies. I thought about how I could leave. I knew that running wasn't an option so, once again I concluded that feigning sanity would be the quickest ticket out. I made sure to interact with the staff and other patients as sanely as I could.

Seven days passed. I was granted a four-hour leave with my family and we went to Christmas dinner at a hotel which was wonderful. The food was excellent and I enjoyed leaving the hospital and seeing a bit of the world outside. There was a buffet with every type of food you could possibly imagine. The feast was incredible. Being off the unit was relieving and lowered my stress levels. After I returned to the unit, everyone was given a present, but I was only given a granola bar and I couldn't figure out the reason for this. The presents were blankets that were nicely wrapped but my granola bar was packaged in a box crudely covered with wrapping paper. I couldn't understand why they didn't care for me and figured they just wanted to encourage me to eat more. I think getting nothing probably would have been better. Luckily, I still trusted the staff, but this could have led me to completely estrange myself from everyone, thinking they didn't genuinely care about me.

One of the major benefits of staying at an excellent psych hospital was being correctly medicated. Before my second episode I was overmedicated but the hospital staff tried different medications, monitored their effects, and determined exactly what I needed. They believed in less medication rather than more, so it took me longer to eliminate symptoms but I still had the energy to do the things I enjoyed. I still take a dose of medication similar to that which I was prescribed during this hospitalization five years ago.

During episodes, I had many delusional behaviors which occurred for illogical reasons that seemed quite logical to me. My delusions mostly revolved around my desire to save the world through righteous behavior. I acted the way I thought everyone should act in order to optimize living conditions for everyone on earth. I was very obdurate in my delusions and was unwilling to listen to anyone who tried persuading me to change, because I felt responsible to help everyone on earth. Many patients who are hospitalized have the same adherence to their beliefs; the doctors and staff have difficulty helping them change unhealthy habits.

My ideal of wanting to do the right thing wasn't bad, but some of my ideas were simply irrational. If someone had shown me good reasons to act in a rational manner which still served the greatest good, then I would have converted to healthier habits. To hear people tell me that my ideas were idealistic, unrealistic, and unattainable inclined me to continue putting them into practice. I didn't want to hear people tell me the world couldn't be saved by my behaviors and I became unwilling to listen to anyone who tried. If people were to have refuted my delusions with rational counterarguments instead of just telling me to dispel my deepest concerns, then I would have been far more willing to change my behaviors. If someone would have informed me there is plenty of food on earth—the problem is that it is spoiling before it arrives in famished areas—then I would have eaten more and wouldn't have starved myself. If someone informed me buying everything organic isn't sustainable economically and the economy needs to persist to perpetuate civilization, then I would have been more willing to use non-organic and non-fair trade items and would have had more clothes to wear during my first episode. I wouldn't have been freezing after donating all my non-organic and non-fair trade clothing. The key to this therapy is that the argument for the healthy behavior needs to be completely true.

Two days later I checked out of in-patient care and transferred to out-patient. The doctor ideally would have kept me a couple more weeks but I was eager to leave and the hospital was short on beds and had other patients who were in greater need of in-patient care than I was. Out-patient care didn't start until the beginning of January, which was a few days away, so I had time to celebrate Christmas late at home with my family.

The out-patient clinic was located at a nearby hospital and was great because it provided a well-structured day focused on therapy. The day began at 8 am with a morning check-in group, followed by a class educating patients about mental health, then lunch. The afternoon consisted of a therapy group where we learned strategies for coping with and solving mental health issues or sometimes played learning games involving mental health information. After, there was a final discussion group and the day ended at 3 pm. While at out-patient I was still psychotic and highly symptomatic. I spoke cryptically, believing that people needed to figure out what I was saying in order to *earn* the knowledge I was conveying. I still made new friends there, and I reunited with the clairvoyant woman who I met during in-patient care. It was nice having someone I could relate to, who understood me, because many of the other patients weren't quite certain how to interact with me.

I was positive to the point where I never mentioned anything that was bothering me and didn't disclose my diagnosis to the group while checking in. Most people do, so that others understand what they've experienced and have a frame of reference. I only participated when I had answers for other people, and one guy started mentioning how he thought *some* people there didn't actually have ailments and were just collecting money from their insurance. He wasn't able to see how disjointed my thoughts were; he wanted to compare illnesses, describing his ailment as a major problem and mine as obviously nonexistent. I was clearly in a dysfunctional state and most everyone else was aware of this and told him so. I didn't want to argue—and I didn't want to mention my illness to anyone—so I kept quiet and let him talk. Sometimes people like comparing problems; their mentality is that the greater their problem is the prouder they should be. In reality, the less problems we have the better, so finding solutions to problems, rather than glorifying the problem itself, fosters optimal living conditions. Talking about a problem in search of a solution is good and helps people find answers, but bragging about a problem is stupid. If you are bragging about an existing problem you clearly haven't solved it yet. You've merely stated that you lack the resourcefulness to find solutions for an ailment. You think being unable to solve problems is a badge of honor while in reality it's not. Bragging about problems creates negative attention and people will perceive you as myopic and incompetent for doing so.

If I trivialize someone else's problems in comparison to my own, it is obviously disrespectful, stupid, and isn't helpful towards finding any solutions. Trivializing other's problems can make them feel insignificant and also suggests that their problem isn't substantial enough for anyone to help them with it. It suggests that they should ignore or endure the problem, which would be detrimental to their well being. It's best to help others when they reach out for help. There have been times when someone has expressed a concern to me which is really related to a deeper concern.

I met one girl who was a cancer patient and didn't know she had cancer. I didn't realize why her head was shaved. I thought she shaved it because she cut it for practical reasons and complimented her on her decision. She knew I was mentally discomposed at the time and was kind about it. She showed me her license picture with her previous look. This incident merely reflects my lack of intuition while I was ill.

Chapter 6
Gaining Ground

At night I was reading and studying as much as possible. I also began going to the gym again. I had far more energy than I did after my first hospitalization because I was taking a lower dose of medication. The main reason I was willing to take my medication was because the quality of my life wasn't completely diminished as it had previously been. The lower dose still left me with some psychotic symptoms, but they were manageable. There were also some side-effects such as drowsiness, a little mental sluggishness and some hunger, but these were far less severe than previously. Regaining my mental functionality without being overwhelmed with the medication's side-effects, I decided to continue taking the medication.

It took a couple months for me to become fully functional again but I eventually regained my sanity without having to sacrifice the quality of my life. As the medication built up in my system the side-effects increased, but after several months I adapted to them. More importantly, the intensity of the side-effects wasn't anywhere near what I had previously experienced, even when they were at their strongest. I was now motivated to take my medication because the sacrifices to regain my sanity were reasonable.

I still had schizoaffective symptoms from taking less medication and these persisted for a while. Though less severe, they were still problematic, but I thought having them was acceptable because I was living a life where I was at least functional and energized and felt this was far better than being amongst the walking dead. I also later realized my symptoms were curable through talk therapy and journaling. These therapies were the "medicine" that eliminated the symptoms.

I asked a professor I'd had during my first episode for a recommendation; I planned to apply to graduate school, thinking I needed the degree in order to become a writer. He asked for a sample of some recent writing and I composed a disjointed essay which was fairly unintelligible. He said he'd be unable to recommend me. I was disappointed because I was uncertain what I would do with my life. I decided to attend a writing class in an adult-education program and pursue writing on my own. The classwork kept me occupied many nights.

One week into out-patient treatment I was allowed to drive again, but I still adhered strictly to the speed limit, afraid I would cause an accident if I went even one mile per hour over the limit. I used my blinkers and drove in the slow lane on the highway. Driving so slowly was actually dangerous, because most people drive at a faster pace. I nearly caused a couple of accidents. On the back roads I was also pretty slow and I nearly caused a few accidents there too. People would stay behind me for minutes at a time, some tailing me and beeping for me to speed up, but I thought I was doing the right thing and stayed below the speed limit. Luckily, I didn't cause any accidents, but I probably shouldn't have been allowed to drive until I was in a better state of mind. (If you have a family member recovering from a mental illness I think you should drive with them until you know they have reached a point where they can safely operate a vehicle.)

Out-patient continued for another week and a half, and afterwards I was allowed to return home. I spent time watching sports and reorganizing the house. I was still attending the writing class and it was one of the only activities I went out for. Sometimes I ran errands with my mom; it was helpful to get out and interact with people, even if only for a few minutes periodically. I began looking forward to errands.

I was still gaining weight since the second hospitalization. I constantly checked the scale but was only 165 lbs and had more weight to gain, which was a lot of fun. I was tired and slept a good amount but not nearly as much as I had after the first hospitalization.

Living at home, I still believed Israel had been nuked and that all of Europe would be experiencing nuclear fallout from the blast. I also thought the US was blockading its borders, keeping out emigrants trying to escape the nuclear fallout. I wouldn't eat any fish. Coincidentally my parents served tilapia and mentioned in conversation that it was a fresh water, farm-raised fish. I thought they were referencing the fact that eating any ocean fish could be harmful, because the ocean fish would be contaminated from nuclear fallout. I was thinking about Europe blanketed in nuclear fall-out and wondering why the world couldn't get along and I got so angry I put my elbow through a wall. My parents were disconcerted and wondered why I did this, but I thought I had to keep the information a secret, believing there were only certain people who knew about the situation. I thought if I informed people about the nuclear fallout, a panic would spread and cause more problems. I was paranoid, expecting that the world was going to end and thinking that each day might be my last. I constantly read the paper, checking for indications of any secret information being conveyed to me through metaphor in the news articles. I eventually eliminated this delusion once I was able to think more rationally, and realized people were still living in Europe and were safe.

It's important to note that I was still having difficulty processing language and clearly articulating my thoughts. Schizoaffective Disorder is a very disorienting mental illness, but the most difficult part about it is the inability to process language coherently. It feels like there is an overload of the subconscious pouring into the conscious, because of the inability to filter and hold thoughts, making the effort to speak feel overwhelming. I would jump from one idea to the next, attempting to create sentences without providing the information which would connect the ideas and make the thoughts coherent. Even today, while I am normally coherent, there are moments when my mind jumps ahead and I say a few words before saying the words that should have come before them. So if I was thinking of saying, "My thoughts are preceding my actions," I might end up saying, "My thoughts are my actions." This has abated as I've progressed more in therapy but it still happens periodically.

I was also having difficulty ingesting language because my mind was filled with racing thoughts, which made it difficult for me to focus on the speaker and process what was being said. I experienced mental weariness and inattentiveness; I would hear bits and pieces of sentences but couldn't fully connect the ideas in the sentences to understand the message being conveyed.

This was a lonely time for me and I began to develop depression. I was upset because my friends from high school weren't returning my calls and I had no one else to turn to. None of them knew there was anything wrong; they probably thought my contentious interactions and mass apologies were merely a reflection of my personality. I didn't want to tell anyone about my illness because I felt embarrassed. I didn't want to admit there was something wrong with me that others had never experienced. I also knew there was a lot of stigma surrounding mental illness and was worried how I would be perceived if people knew I had an illness. (That is still something I worry about today.) I continued reading and writing while at home, and I continued attending my writing group, but outside of these activities I was fairly inactive and felt lame because of it.

I met with a new psychotherapist who was a psychologist and had a separate psychopharmacologist to prescribe medication. He was located close by and was a specialist for psychotic disorders. We made some progress during our meetings but I didn't learn much. After the first few sessions I encountered some problems. During my episodes, many embarrassing things had happened to me because of mental illness and a part of therapy is talking about these occurrences and finding alleviation from them. This psychologist spoke of his pride in his military service, his honorable discharge, his graduation from his master's program, and some other accolades. He was self-righteous and seemed judgmental, so I decided not to discuss any of my issues with him. My mom recommended seeing a psychiatrist at the major psych hospital at which I had recently stayed. I decided this would be for the best. And it was.

During my first visit with this new doctor my time was split between myself and my parents and was more informational than anything else. He talked with them to gain a sense of my past and to learn about my previous symptoms, behaviors, and my overall state of being at this point. He also talked with them so they could meet him and gain an understanding of his personality and goals for therapy.

This doctor is still my doctor and I have learned a lot from our sessions. He is affable and expresses emotion when necessary; I think this is important because it removes the gravity from the meetings. Occasionally he'll ask questions from an objective standpoint when he needs an honest answer. My other doctors had been somewhat austere and our sessions were extremely solemn and almost too much to handle. My current doctor is lighthearted and positive, and this facilitates the broaching of serious issues. Sometimes we joke during sessions and I understand that he cares for my well-being. Overall, I think it's important to monitor your progress with doctors because ultimately some are better qualified than others, just as some human beings have better intellect and higher competencies in some areas than others. Also, different personalities gel better with others. It's important to find the doctor who works best for you. My first doctor seemed wonderful when I first met him but I wound up experiencing a second episode mostly because he was unable to recognize my symptoms, over-medicated me, and abruptly ended our sessions.

I spent our first few visits being terse and unwilling to volunteer much information. We talked about how many conversations occur because people are willing to volunteer information about themselves, but that was something I was unwilling to do. I was so critical of others while they were talking that I thought that same criticism would be returned when I spoke, which made me extremely self-conscious. My self-consciousness made me very quiet. I was also afraid of what people would think of me if they knew about all my strange experiences during episodes. I had developed a habit of keeping as quiet as possible.

Sometimes I would be speaking about a subject and simultaneously think of a delusional thought or a time during an episode where I yelled at someone or ignored someone; it made me afraid of saying something that would disclose that I had a mental illness. For example, I was talking with someone about how a local professional team had won a championship recently. During my episodes, I spent a great deal of time in isolation and never listened to the radio or watched TV, so I had no idea which team had won. The person I was talking with asked if I had seen the championship. I obviously hadn't but I did know the local team won. I could have simply responded by saying I wasn't much of a fan at the time, and the conversation could then have been progressed to a different subject. By stating that I wasn't much of a fan, I wouldn't have been mentioning anything about isolation or episodes; I wouldn't have disclosed any personal information. But I was thinking about how I hadn't watched TV at the time because I was in the middle of an episode and I worried that someone would learn about my mental illness just from my admitting, "I haven't watched TV in the past few months." The speaker then asked why I hadn't watched TV in the past few months and this led to more awkward questions. His questioning lead me to believe that he suspected I had mental illness when in reality he was just curious why I had not watched TV in the past few months, which might seem odd to many people.

I needlessly worried that he knew about my illness when in fact he was merely wondering why I hadn't watched TV. One thing most people don't realize is that there are many people with mental illnesses who are fully functional and interacting with them daily. The only way this guy would have known I had been in an episode when the big game was played was if I had explicitly told him so.

I didn't know that although the episodes were fresh in my mind they were non-existent in most people's minds. The only way they would learn anything about me was if I told them about myself. Reticence is a useful skill to develop; it takes time but it gets easier the more it's practiced. There were many embarrassing occurrences during my episodes that I didn't want people knowing about, but at first it was difficult to keep them to myself. The past four years of my life had been spent in psychosis and my experiences were fresh in my mind. When someone broached a subject, my mind jumped immediately to a relevant psychotic behavior, because my episodes were my most recent experiences and came to mind quicker than anything else.

(Even more recently, when reminded of my past experiences I've had stronger emotional responses and more vivid memories, because my episodes are fresher in my mind from having ruminated about them while writing this memoir. When I'm not working on anything illness-related I usually don't think much about mental illness at all, because I have lived in a healthier state of being within for the past several years and I have had good memories I can share with others while socializing.)

Besides reticence, another technique that would have facilitated socializing and helped me better assimilate would have been educating myself about current events and immersing myself in activities and interests I genuinely enjoy and can talk about with others. I enjoy watching sports but during my episodes I hadn't watched them much at all; researching some local teams and learning how they were doing would have given me more to think and talk about. Taking some trips to museums would have also helped because I love art. I also could have gone to a show or game, or watched movies. If I reconnected myself with subjects other than mental illness I would have had more to talk about with others, instead of revisiting traumatic past memories in conversation.

After a month or so of therapy I was still completely alone and my mom persisted in requesting that I tell my friends I had an illness. She hoped they would understand my contentious and odd behavior and reconnect with me. She went ahead and spoke to them about the illness, and some of them took time to hang out with me again. It was great to get out. In instances where people have experienced something inexplicably awkward, it's helpful to let them know about your illness. Many people had a negative perception of me because of my odd and contentious behavior with them during that second episode. It took time for them to understand I had a mental illness, but word spread and I was able to reconnect with old acquaintances. Many conversations were still fairly awkward, but people were willing to talk to me and I was beginning to reconnect.

But not everyone needs to know about the mental illness. Usually people attribute awkward behaviors and delusional thoughts to personality quirks and don't think much of them. During my second episode, I adamantly encouraged people to drive under the speed limit while in their car. In one instance, I persisted for nearly twenty minutes during a car ride with a friend and he eventually listened but found it odd. Three years later this friend jokingly mentioned how I used to persist in asking him to drive under the speed limit. He was someone who knew about my mental illness but never actually connected my obsession with the speed limit to mental illness. Most people, who are unfamiliar with mental illness, won't make those connections either. Besides, those who can make the connection are well-versed in psychology and are usually understanding people who won't disparage you or put you in an awkward situation.

There were times shortly after my episode where I informed people that certain thoughts I'd expressed were illness-related, and they were surprised and unable to connect the delusions to mental illness. Our conversations became awkward, because I was mentioning at an inappropriate time something that had happened several months, a year, or even several years earlier. The time was inappropriate because when people are out in group social settings they usually convey information that is light, easy to talk about, and fairly impersonal. Usually, when people say strange things or do something odd, the conversation is moved forward; the unusual comment is quickly forgotten and almost never revisited. This means that years later it does not need to be revisited at all, which was something I was unaware of. The awkwardness was due to my revisiting a past situation, which in my mind was still important, because I was thinking about it, but to most people was insignificant and barely remembered if at all. If the people did remember the irrational behaviors and delusional thoughts, they must have left them behind because they were hanging out with me. I could tell by their reactions they thought it was awkward that I felt compelled to revisit these experiences and explain them.

It also left them wondering why I was so hung up on these fairly trivial past occurrences. Just the fact that I remembered the odd behavior and brought it to their attention was odd in itself and created some awkward reactions. Not having spent time with these friends in a while, I attributed my previous estrangement from them to my delusional thoughts and the irrational behavior I'd displayed. I wanted them to know these things wouldn't be happening again. All that was true but mentioning it created distance between us. The best practice for me in situations like that has been to leave such occurrences behind.

There are other groups of friends who I can talk to about almost anything, but this group was different, and it's important to gauge your listeners. The fact that they had decided to hang out with me meant they had already accepted or forgotten those awkward occurrences. The best way to inform people that I was in good health again would have been simply to interact with them and allow my rationality and sanity to present itself in our interactions. My need to reassure them made me socially awkward and my friends began avoiding me again. My phone calls weren't being returned. An important part of my therapy was learning to socialize again. I had been isolated for the past few years so many socialization skills I had previously known were completely gone.

Not very long after that inauspicious beginning, I was interacting coherently and people mentioned how they enjoyed my company, all without my mentioning any mental health problems. As a result, I made new friends and hung out with old friends more regularly again.

My days lacked structure and I struggled to keep busy. I was looking for full-time work but was unable to find anything because I was a recent college grad with no experience who was entering a work force plagued by a recession. I looked for part time work and eventually found a job stocking shelves at a local store. When you are looking for work, having a job opens doors for other interviews because employers like seeing that you are working, regardless of where you're employed. Having a job shows you are punctual, diligent, dependable, and willing to work, and you are spending your time usefully.

While applying for work I didn't inform my prospective employers of my mental illness, unless I was applying for a government job. I always prefer not to. People say they'll give equal opportunity to those with disabilities, but there are still people who have stigmatic perceptions of those with mental illness. I thought if there was one place where disclosing my mental illness would help me get a job it would be psychology, but so far, I've been mistaken. I applied to five or six different mental health clinics to work as a mental health specialist on a unit. I disclosed my illness in all my applications, thinking it would be a great credential. The mental health specialist is someone who interacts with the patients daily, talks to them about their issues, and facilitates discussion groups. It doesn't require a psych degree and they hire people from a variety of backgrounds to fill this position. At the time I applied for these jobs, I was (and still am) lecturing Harvard Medical School Resident Doctors four times a year. My essays have been published in Oxford University medical journals. Yet out of the five or six mental health clinics I applied to, not one even replied to my application. It could be possible that there were better qualified candidates in each of the situations, but it's odd that they all turned down someone with eight years of empirical knowledge of schizoaffective disorder, when many of their applicants have little to no mental health experience whatsoever.

Some employers are afraid employees with psychotic disorders could be a liability and will avoid hiring them, especially if the work requires intellect. Some will discriminate against those with mental illnesses and decide not to hire them while outwardly citing other plausible reasons for not hiring those applicants, as a cover. There are usually many candidates applying for the same position who have comparable abilities and employers can easily find plausible reasons to hire a person who does not have a mental illness over someone who does.

I was still extremely lonely but I was going to work, and interacting with others was very helpful. I was conversing affably at work and doing so boosted my self-esteem; if I could get along with these people I could get along with others too and eventually make friends. For the first time in months I had a schedule and was regularly getting out of the house and putting energy towards a positive goal. The work itself was also beneficial because there was a lot of walking and there were many heavy items to lift which helped keep me in shape. Work also eliminated some of the lameness I had felt from being so inactive during the previous months. It felt good getting a paycheck and earning my own money money instead of having to borrow it. I weighed nearly 210 lbs at this time and was well over-weight, mostly due to depression.

I was progressing in therapy and was beginning to face my problems, which took courage. I had been fairly quiet for the first of couple months of therapy, pre-ferring to completely ignore my mental illness and all the problems surrounding it. Thinking about my issues was painful and my initial reaction was to avoid painful experiences, which most people do. I made progress on some of the smaller issues in my life but continued to withhold information about my worst ailments.

Another challenge I faced was overcoming de-nial. Part of me still wanted to believe there was nothing wrong in my life. I thought if I continued moving forward my problems would be left in my wake, but that didn't happen. Many of my problems stuck with me and even got worse until I faced them and resolved them. I also had the impression that most people don't have prob-lems in their lives, but that is false. Most people have problems and if they're working toward solutions they usually do that work on their own or with those who are close to them; they don't usually disclose their private lives in social situations. This can lead you to believe no one has any problems, but most people have imperfect lives. People who tell you everything is perfect in their lives are usually hiding their issues, either because their problems are personal and/or painful, or because the person is in denial. Yet another reason for pretend-ing everything is fine is because sharing problems can dampen a conversation.

I began attending a talk group at the hospital. The group consisted of other patients who weren't as functional as I was and I found it difficult to relate to them because we were at different points in our therapy. Many of these people were stagnant in their recovery and it could be triggering to be with them. I did enjoy talking with people who I could share my experiences with, but I was also looking for friends, and I was unable to meet anyone I could hang out with. I stopped attending the group after a month, because I found that being with patients who were not progressing in their therapy was more detrimental than beneficial.

After stocking shelves for a month, I found full-time employment in a major hotel chain as a front desk agent. Working full-time was beneficial for me because I was interacting with people on a regular basis and had structure to my day. Unfortunately, my social life was non-existent, because I worked many nights and weekends and the schedule was created only a couple days before the beginning of the week and was constantly rotating, which made it very difficult to plan anything. Even when friends did call me I was usually unable to hang out, and I couldn't plan any recurring activities, such as weekly writing groups, because of the changing schedule. It was a small hotel and they needed as much out of everyone as they could get. I checked to see if there were opportunities to advance. The next job required 55 hours as opposed to the 40 hours I was currently working, and the schedule was no less unpredictable. So I decided I would start looking elsewhere for employment. I was becoming depressed because of my loneliness. I worked at the hotel until September, when I found a job with an insurance carrier. I began working at my new job in October.

Over the years, I had become resentful for the wrongs that had been inflicted on me; now I blamed my depression on all the bad things that people had done to me. I had my own faults I needed to address but found it easier to blame my unhappiness on the actions of others.

I eventually realized I needed to be forgiving, because there is a great amount of good which results from it. My therapist tells me if we were all judged for our worst moments we would live in a pretty awful world; *most* people would be considered bad human beings. I agree with him. Forgiveness is an essential part of life and being forgiving makes a great difference. Some people harp on vengeance but vengeance only creates a cycle of wrongdoing in which both parties are at fault. People who are vengeful are constantly afraid there will be retribution if they make any mistakes, because they are so accustomed to retaliating when others wrong them they expect the same in return. Fear arrests thinking and makes life more difficult for those who are unwilling to forgive. Being able to forgive has allowed me to drop the emotional baggage I was carrying as a result of feeling wronged. When I began forgiving people for the wrongs they did, I was able to see them at their best and remember the good times we had experienced. My perception changed and I realized we have all made mistakes and have wronged one another, but for the most part, the people I felt resentful towards were good people. After deciding to forgive I began reconnecting with old friends who I had been avoiding. To this day, I still hang out with many of them and have a great time.

Most importantly, I was still resentful towards my parents, blaming them for problems that weren't their fault. Having lately discovered that they were only human—not the perfect people I had imagined them to be—I began to blame them for the derision I'd experienced when I was younger. Because I'd spent so much time with them, I'd picked up certain of their quirks and characteristics. I noticed myself exhibiting the same quirks during my episodes, and decided those inherited mannerisms must have been the reason that people made fun of me. In truth, the derision I'd experienced was due to my having a cognitive impairment and being unable to coherently interact with others. I decided it wasn't their fault and set out to repair our relationship. I also realized I simply had to forgive them for the things that had actually been their fault, and understand that they did their absolute best. No one is perfect, including myself. The reparation of our relationship was helpful for me. Holding a grudge against the people who cared most about me had created a lot of stress. The elimination of the grudge also eliminated the subconscious guilt I felt about turning away from people who had been so good to me for my entire life.

Much of my therapy focused on my fear of being lonely. I was afraid of losing my friends again; I had not gotten over the pain of losing all my friends during my first episode, in college, and while in middle school. It took courage to attempt making friends but if I didn't try, my only option was loneliness. And that wasn't working. I had nothing to lose.

That November I ran into some friends who I had lived with at the fraternity; they had learned about my mental illness. They told me that they hadn't known what was wrong during the first episode. They didn't know how to help me back then because I was so un-approachable and they didn't understand what was happening. We talked and hung out the entire night. I felt relieved that these people didn't hate me. There have been many other times where I have seen old ac-quaintances, and they have also shown genuine inter-est in my well-being, wishing the best for me. So this entire time I'd been concerned about people hating me while they were actually genuinely concerned for me and glad to learn I was doing well. I thought I had some good reasons to support my belief that they hated me, but all of the contentious interactions I was so concerned about had been completely forgotten.

Chapter 7
Talk Therapy and Journaling

Medication was useful for stabilizing me and limiting some of my symptoms, but talk therapy has been the most important medicine for helping me cure my mental illness. I discovered that the roots of my problems were negative and traumatic psychological experiences, some of which had happened during my episodes, and others that had happened earlier in my life, due to the difficulty of growing up with a cognitive impairment. Talking about issues enabled me to find relief from ailments lodged in my subconscious which were affecting me constantly.

When I began talk therapy I was having difficulty speaking even the shortest of sentences. I made enough progress to gain employment in telephone customer service. Eventually I became comfortable speaking to anyone, and I currently enjoy a vibrant social life. The first thing my talk therapist did was develop rapport. I was in talk therapy because I had many deeply traumatizing experiences that I needed to disclose and analyze in detail. It was already difficult enough to face the issues that frightened and traumatized me the most, without having to relate them to someone who seemed to be judging me for having them. My episodes and the years I'd lived through left me with negative emotions such as anxiety and fear, and an important part of therapy was determining the thoughts causing these emotions.

I had many delusions acquired from years of cognitive impairment as well as delusions developed during my episodes, all of which contributed to my stress and neurosis. I had always found it difficult to talk about my deepest feelings, even to people I had known my whole life, never mind to a complete stranger. That is why my current doctor's friendliness was helpful in encouraging me to talk. His kindness assured he was on my side. I have had therapists who have been austere, who I didn't make progress with, and therapists who have been friendly, to whom I am forever grateful, because they helped me progress beyond horizons I previously could not have imagined.

My austere psychiatrists exuded judgement, while my current psychiatrist is a guide who allows me to think and listens to my thoughts and gives occasional advice when necessary. The judgmental therapists were difficult to work with because I made mistakes during episodes, did many strange things, and had many issues I needed to share which, outside of therapy, would be completely taboo socially. When I felt I was going to be judged I was far more careful about disclosing information. However, with my current therapist, who from the start has been someone who is there to help and is always on my side, I felt it was safe to disclose my deepest and most hidden thoughts. He created a positive and friendly environment which encouraged me to talk and helped me to face difficult issues. My therapist kept the conversations positive, which gave me a positive attitude and a hopeful outlook. He made it seem possible to overcome my mental illness, which created an inclination for progress. The attitude which works best for me is to understand that we are talking about ailments in order to solve problems, not to lament. Because of the mind set he helped to foster, I have never felt as though I am complaining during our sessions together.

Even with this new therapist, I withheld some problems from experiences in my first episode which I had been thinking about for years. It took two years of therapy for me to finally trust him enough to disclose the problems. After disclosing this information, I came to realize my problems were common for someone with schizoaffective disorder and I didn't have anything to be afraid of. I think it's important to have the courage to divulge your secrets to your therapist because doing so is immensely beneficial. There are also many issues people think are particular to themselves but are actually common for people with their particular mental illness.

After overcoming these issues, I began progressing a great deal.

It's important to understand that you can divulge your secrets to whoever you want, but you can also withhold them from anyone too. Identifying and talking about your problems with one person doesn't mean anyone else will ever know anything about your conversation.

In therapy, I do most of the talking and my therapist guides me towards answers I have trouble finding. There are occasions when he flat out disagrees with me, but I am willing to listen when this happens, because he also listens to me. There is a give and take in the conversation, which makes me feel as though I am contributing and my thoughts are important. This also allows him to disagree with me when he needs to say something crucial for my well-being. When I have been preached to or lectured at in talk therapy, I felt my thoughts were far less valuable and contributed less to the conversation.

There were times when I developed a dependence on my psychotherapists, but later on I realized that I myself am the person who needs to do most of the work of healing. Psychiatrists are helpful and can help with major issues, but there are too many problems in life for me to be completely dependent upon another person to solve them. I need to think through issues on my own. I know that the more I have solved problems on my own the better I have become at it. This is useful because I can only meet with a psychotherapist for one hour per week while I am on my own for the rest of the week. Even if I did want to ask my therapist for help on every problem in my life there simply wouldn't be enough time.

I have been my own best asset in therapy because I have a record of all my experiences in my mind and I am the one experiencing the feelings of the trauma. I am the one who had the information which needed to be worked with to alleviate my troubles, and the disclosure of this information only began once I was encouraged to talk. I have also known when the right "medicinal words" have been hit upon, because I have felt the alleviation from those words as soon as I have understood them. Talking with the therapist and being proactive in therapy is important because there have been many times I have been able to resolve issues without visiting my therapist. There have been other times where I wasn't able to resolve them but did gather information regarding them. Once I shared this information with my therapist we were able to find resolutions for the problems I was facing. My talk therapist forced me to think through and answer the questions I had about my issues and created a positive environment which enabled me to develop the right attitude towards psychology. He asked me the questions I needed to ask myself. My being able to answer these questions made me realize I have agency, I can help myself, and I can make my life the way I want it to be. This realization was important because it motivated me to make changes in my life. Developing problem-solving skills took time, but as my skills evolved, the power I held over my life also increased.

Anyone can develop problem solving-skills. I think it's essential for psychotherapists to help their patients to become their own best resource. I developed such a liking for getting results through therapy that I eventually started journaling. I psychoanalyze myself in my journal and work through issues; this has helped me to progress much faster than I could if I just waited for one hour of therapy per week.

Schizoaffective disorder can be a difficult illness to combat because there are life experiences prior to the illness that may have caused trauma but there is also a network of thoughts, delusions, implied thoughts and implied delusions that are created from the patient's experiences during episodes, which cause stress, anxiety, and paranoia after the episodes. A "clear" delusion and/or thought is a sentence that has actually been verbalized in the mind and is clearly identified as something that may be bothering someone or is something they are afraid of. An implied delusion or thought is when there are a series of events and there is trauma resulting from those events and someone has subconsciously drawn a conclusion as a result of their experience but hasn't actually verbalized or consciously identified it. In talk therapy and journaling I work to root out these thoughts and pacify them.

Stress was one of the key elements that triggered my psychotic symptoms and diminished the quality of my life, so my main goal in talk therapy has been eliminating as much stress as possible. This is done by talking about issues from any time in my life, finding and eliminating delusions, and creating plans to improve my social life or any other facet of my life I have felt is insufficient. The alleviation of stress from any and all sources has been the main reason for the alleviation of my psychotic symptoms such as referential thinking, auditory hallucinations, and paranoia. Referential thinking and paranoia were a direct result of having poor self-esteem and having traumatic experiences during episodes; talk therapy helped changed my self-perception. With my doctor's help, I also transformed the meaning surrounding the traumatic experiences, which alleviated their burden. My auditory hallucinations always occurred after or during my most stressful days, but once I was able to eliminate stress from trauma and delusions I did not experience auditory hallucinations as often. At present I have them no more than once every several months.

There were times when I was feeling emotions that I was unable to eliminate, but talk therapy helped me find the thoughts causing these emotions and diffuse them. Sometimes present situations made me feel anxiety or fear, and my anxiety and fear caused neurosis. These emotions were caused by thoughts lodged in my subconscious from past trauma which I needed to identify. The emotions had such a palpability and presence in my consciousness that they actually restricted and limited my intelligence during social situations, because it is more difficult to think while experiencing emotions such as fear and anxiety.

There is a tendency to avoid thoughts that create negative emotions, but part of therapy is facing these thoughts. When you have to think about the cause of your fear or anxiety, it can sometimes create more anxiety and fear. Understanding that thinking about these things will improve my life has motivated me to persist while feeling uncomfortable emotions.

Sometimes just facing trauma can be difficult but it's important to come to honest terms with experiences and call them exactly what they are. Calling something by its name eliminates some of the fear surrounding it and normalizes it; it is mentally liberating.

It was sometimes difficult to be honest with myself because some experiences that I had during my episodes were emotionally painful to think about, but

I've found it's better to give myself the truth, regardless of how painful it might be, rather than tell myself the things I wanted to hear. All of our experience is record-ed somewhere in our minds, and that record is always going to reflect the truth about things we've experi-enced. When I've been honest with myself, I've come to realizations about my experiences that I wasn't able to arrive at before, because I previously wasn't willing to give myself the information I needed to hear. Hearing the truth helped me create the outcome I wanted from therapy: liberation from the effects of trauma and opti-mizing my functionality.

The most difficult facet of having a psychological issue is knowing there is something within your sub-conscious that frightens or bothers you but being un-able to identify it. One of my therapist's most essential functions has been helping me identify the issues af-fecting me, because when we have identified issues they have been extremely easy to eliminate. I've come to understand that, to identify an issue, I have to be completely honest with myself, even if it may cause me pain. The truth is forever lodged in my psyche; if I am unwilling to admit what it is, I can't accurately determine what is truly bothering me and find alleviation from it. For a while I had a tendency to ignore the issues that were most painful which is something I believe most people do naturally. For me it was a defense mecha-nism against re-living traumatic experiences, but was also habitual. Over the years, I completely pushed cer-tain issues out of my mind on a regular basis and I had to change the habit of doing so when I finally decided to address those issues. I now look for my most painful issues because I understand I can alleviate the burden they are creating once I know what they are. There are times where I find myself procrastinating while thinking about an issue, and this usually indicates to me that this issue has significance within my psyche. Just the fact that there is fear surrounding that issue has informed me it is psychologically damaging and needs to be addressed, and this encourages me to continue addressing it.

Talk therapy is important because the therapist helps guide the patient to information that helps identify and understand the thoughts causing the negative emotions. Once I understand the thoughts causing the emotions I am able to find logic to defuse the thought causing the anxiety or fear. In therapy the goal is to make the thoughts surrounding the traumatic experiences a zero or a positive. Usually while thinking of zeros people might consider them to be something with no meaning, but I consider a zero to be something which has no effect on me in any way, which means I can think a thought or perform an everyday action without experiencing any negative repercussions from doing so. Transforming something that was awful into something that is positive has been very empowering.

For example, I was afraid to befriend anyone for a while, because I had lost all my friends during my first episode and at other junctions in my life. Once I understood that the loss of those friends was the reason I was afraid to befriend more people, I worked to find reasons why I wouldn't lose new friends when I made them. I eventually realized there were major differences in my personality at age 19, when I was friendless, and at present, when I am a very likable person. I understood that I had lost friends because of my illness but I also realized that my illness is fully under control at this point. I will most likely never have another episode. I am familiar with my symptoms and know when to get help to prevent another episode. Besides, there are people in my life who are familiar with my symptoms— my doctor, who I see weekly, and my family— and I know they will intervene if I need help and have reached a point where I am unwilling to help myself or admit I need any help. These thoughts pacified my fears of losing friends and encouraged me to try making friends.

Discussing the logistics of socializing with friends, dating, and functionally interacting with others was very important for me. I had been isolated for a long time before reentering the social world and there was a lot I didn't understand about socializing. I had forgotten and was completely out of touch with social norms, expectations, and codes of conduct. After experiencing two and a half years of psychosis I had no idea of what was socially or culturally acceptable, but my therapist gave me the answers to questions I was unable to ask others. Sometimes I would pace rapidly outside of his office, other times I would laugh out loud in public by myself, and other times I would not respond to people after being spoken to — I wouldn't have known I was doing anything wrong if no one had informed me. Everything I had remembered from earlier years had completely changed, because I was at a different stage of my life and people had matured. Talking about the nuances of social interaction helped me figure out what was socially acceptable and not socially acceptable, and gave me a sense of how to get along better with others. We discussed expectations for social situations, which enabled me to prepare mentally for different social situations.

Although these discussions were helpful, just getting out and participating in social situations was the most essential part in learning how to socialize. I reflected on my experiences on my own and with my doctor and determined which things were working, and also learned how I could improve in other areas. I was able to bring back data points to my doctor, which was essential in my improvement. Even when I wasn't able to figure things out for myself, bringing back information about my interactions helped my doctor to better understand my situation and my psyche. Simply from having more information about me, he was able to help improve my life, because he gained a better understanding of me.

Being in talk therapy helped me start talking again. After I said even the strangest of things, my therapist gave a warm response to validate my thoughts, which encouraged me to talk and informed me that I was someone worth listening to.

I have learned so much about life and about myself from psychotherapy and have immensely benefited from the ideas discussed and taught during sessions. I have found peace by discussing issues and finding solutions which medication can't provide. It took time for me to reach a point where I felt rehabilitated, but I am currently past that point and have been continually improving. Medication helps the brain mechanically function but psychotherapy helps the person solve the problems the illness created (and many more). I understand that I need to attend psychotherapy sessions for the rest of my life in order to refill prescriptions but I'm grateful for that. If my illness were suddenly eliminated and I had the option of declining talk therapy, I would still go, because I benefit so much from it. Many people don't have someone they can talk to about life but I have someone who has been trained to deal with life issues. I feel fortunate. There are many times where I'll talk about issues which are completely independent of my illness and I look forward to having someone to talk to about anything I want every week for an hour.

After my third year of therapy I began writing in a

metacognitive journal. Journaling about my issues was paramount in my recovery from schizoaffective disorder. As I've mentioned, a difficult part of facing my fears was being in the habit of protecting myself from them and hiding them.

There have been times where I've begun broaching a subject and then found myself two rooms away from my notebook, trying to preoccupy myself with another activity. When I find myself avoiding a fear that I've recently discovered or identified, I try to do my best to sit myself down and face it. The fact that a certain subject is causing me to procrastinate means I've been avoiding it for a while, possibly because it is particularly painful, but I attack it because I know I'll find alleviation by facing it. After identifying these negative experiences, I then ask myself: how are they currently affecting me and making me feel? And how is this influencing my life? Ultimately the meaning I have assigned to my past experiences determines how they affect me.

I found thoughts to write in my journal that refuted past delusions that were restricting, and created parameters that would help me socialize better. I faced and thought through irrational fears I have had to completely eliminate them. I also worked with changing the meaning I had attached to certain experiences and worked to gain a better perspective on my life. I wrote down thoughts that gave me confidence or showed me instances where I experienced the thing or situation I was afraid of and did well. The most powerful thoughts written in my journal were those that addressed fears from trauma and refuted them with empirical knowledge, demonstrating how I had already faced my fears and overcome them.

I continue to do this kind of work in my journal. I also write down social insights which give me a better sense of how to interact, precepts, better ways to think and communicate. But most importantly I use my journal to identify the things I am afraid of. One of the most difficult parts of trauma is being afraid of something and not knowing what exactly it is. Keeping a journal has cleared space in my mind to write about a fear and analyze that particular fear. Once it's on paper, it is easier to work with; I am able to delve deeper into the issue. Also, writing thoughts in my journal somehow makes those thoughts permanently accessible within my mind —even though they are written down and are no longer in the forefront of my mind.

For example, for quite some time I was afraid of people knowing I have schizoaffective disorder. I thought if people knew I had schizoaffective disorder they might think I wasn't cool enough to hang out with them, or they might be influenced by the stigma that popular culture attaches to the illness and think I was unstable and unsafe to be around. To challenge this thought I wrote "Having schizoaffective disorder does not affect my personality." When I wrote that in my journal, I realized that my friends would only judge me for the person they knew me as and wouldn't just leave me because they were informed I have schizoaffective disorder. I also realized that I should only tell people I have the illness once they gain an unbiased perception of who I am and can see that I am not my illness and I am a person just like anyone else.

I was able to eliminate past fears mostly through exposure therapy. I subjected myself to my fears in small doses and then analyzed the experiences through reflection and recorded my findings in my journal. I found what worked and what I needed to improve on and determined what I needed to do to function better in certain situations, mostly social situations. Having some success in situations I had been afraid of eliminated a lot of fears for me.

The experiences I reflect on to build my confidence are limited to things that have happened since my episodes, because I consider myself a different person before and after the episodes. The experiences I had before my episodes are irrelevant because I was functioning differently before I developed the illness as opposed to after.

Sometimes I have precise thoughts to address particular issues but there have been other times when it is not so clear. I have had to search and find out the reasons why I am having issues. When I've had to search my psyche to determine what has been bothering me, I usually use probing thoughts based on my best guess of what the pith of the matter is. I've developed these hypotheses from knowing what my most traumatic experiences have been, determining the meaning assigned to those experiences, and then figuring out how that meaning is affecting me in present day situations. Usually there has been a common element in the present-day situation and the traumatic experience. After writing down these thoughts, I have assessed how I have felt afterwards. Self-assessment has been a critical facet of determining whether a thought written in my journal is helpful or is detrimental. When I have found a thought I have written in my journal hasn't helped my mind to function better, I have crossed it out, telling myself to completely disregard it, and I've continued on. When I have found an idea that has worked I have kept it.

Having life goals to work towards was an essential part of my therapy. It was important for me to figure out what I wanted in life and then create plans and talk about ways I could make these goals a reality. Some things I wanted in life were a job, friends, a girlfriend, and a meaningful life. Improving my functionality through talk therapy and journaling was an essential part of obtaining my goals. The improvement in my psyche helped me to function better socially and eliminated a lot of my social anxiety. Seeing how the improvement in my psyche helped improve my social interactions motivated me to work harder, because I realized my life had changed for the better. Experiencing improvements which brought me closer to my life goals gave me hope that these therapies could help me obtain the things I wanted out of life. This improved my mood immensely because my goals were—and still are—the things that create happiness for me. Knowing I could obtain them just by working in therapy made a huge difference. It was empowering; I had felt my efforts were somewhat futile until I was able to see therapy was making a useful impact on my life.

Initially progress was slow and I didn't push too hard because I was becoming comfortable talking about issues that were difficult to face. As my well-being improved I increased my expectations and continued raising the bar for myself; I eventually progressed well beyond recovery, and I am still working to become a better functioning person daily. Talk therapy takes tenacity and it isn't an overnight process. It was more of a marathon for me but was well worth running. I continually worked to improve and as my health improved I became better at identifying and changing the residual delusions and odd behaviors lodged in my subconscious. This improved the quality of my life immensely and also improved my socialization skills. Most of the progress I have made and will continue to make through psychotherapy has been a result of talk therapy and journaling, and most of my symptoms of paranoia and neurosis have been completely alleviated. It has taken time and tenacity, but I have made progress with each session and journal entry.

These are the words I have come to live by: "*To*

improve is to change; to be perfect is to change often." (Winston Churchill)

Chapter 8
Lessons I've Learned

Many people think differently of you if they know you have been to a psych hospital and it takes time for them to overcome the stigma society attaches to mental illness. My initial interactions with people who had learned about my second hospitalization were somewhat awkward. They tried being as nice as possible, which was well-meant, but they were skirting the issue, making an effort to completely avoid saying anything at all that might upset me in even the slightest way. They avoided making any sort of negative or disparaging comment, even if it had nothing to do with mental health. They eventually began treating me just like any other person but it took time. In my case, it was helpful for some people to know about my mental health. However, if I can withhold this information I usually do. I prefer being treated the way any other person would be.

The stigma attached to mental illness generates fear and fosters the thought that mentally ill people are lower quality human beings who are unpredictable; most people don't realize there are many people who have mental illnesses who are upstanding citizens functionally interacting with them daily. There was an instance where I was talking to a new acquaintance and she asked if I knew her friend from my town. I did, so she texted him. I read his response, which stated that I "should be in an asylum". This hurt and I was unable to conceal my angst and humiliation. She knew I had mental health issues and after that she was unwilling to talk to me. What had been a twenty-minute conversation abruptly halted; from then on, she and her friends avoided me. During the earlier part of the party they'd spoken frequently with me. She was clearly myopic but it was painful to know some people will avoid me just because I have a mental disorder.

At a different party about a year later, I encountered the person who had texted the girl, saying I should be in the asylum. My first impulse was to say something or to cause him some trouble but I knew it wouldn't do any good. I realized the only way to repair my reputation with him would be to engage him in a normal conversation, so I did. The conversation went well and we had a few laughs. I'm uncertain whether it fully changed his perception of me but I know it helped. This is my practice with all people who I determine have some sort of prejudice against me for having a mental illness, because it helps them to realize that this person who has a mental illness is just as good as anyone else.

When I run into people who I know have a strange or negative perception of me I do my best to engage them in cordial conversation for at least a couple minutes. I do this because it's polite but but also because it may change their perception. These are usually people who I've had disjointed conversations with during my episodes or people I yelled at when we lived together at the fraternity. I simply relax and try to be myself with them. I know I am a good person who is fairly rational, but I also know that episodic behavior may have led people to think otherwise. Reframing their perspective of me with positive interactions has been helpful in reconnecting with old acquaintances who previously felt deterred from speaking to me. Usually if I talk to someone and they can see I am coherent, and they enjoy my company, they'll dispel their previous perception or biases and they'll hang out with me. This has happened a number of times.

I was at a party once and a friend who was bipolar wanted to talk to me about mental health issues. This was one of the first times someone had decided to openly engage me in mental health conversation around others and I was uncertain of how to interact. I answered his questions and contributed to the conversation, but the people surrounding us were a little disconcerted and many of them left the area we were talking in. I felt some embarrassment and decided this is something I am no longer going to do. There are still times when people want to publicly engage me in conversations about mental illness and and I assess the situation. If I'm in a cafe in a one-on-one conversation and talking quietly I don't mind it, but if I'm in a more communal environment such as a party or social outing I'll defer the conversation to a later time to save us from judgement. It's also quite awkward discussing personal problems to someone in public because these matters are best left private. People generally go out to have fun and don't feel like dealing with serious issues while they're out. Most people hide their problems from the general public and if they are around people who are talking openly about serious issues they feel quite awkward. On a separate note, some people talk about these issues openly for attention—but they are only drawing negative attention. Negative attention is detrimental.

While deferring the conversation to a later time I try to ensure that I don't reveal any information about myself; I immediately inform the person that we can talk later. Others may assume there was a reason the person was asking me about mental health, but if they don't know me they may think I am a mental health professional, or they may assume I am just a friend who knows something about my friend and is the person they usually talk to. If they are smart enough to figure it out they are usually conscientious enough to keep quiet.

While I was sleeping over at a friend's house,

she noticed me taking medication and asked me what it was for. At this point, there was no covering up the medication so I told her it was for insomnia. The medication does help me sleep but I also know insomnia is a far more socially acceptable illness than schizoaffective disorder and people don't think of me any differently when they're informed I have insomnia. Some people are actually intrigued, for whatever reason.

I usually withhold illness-related information altogether, but there have been times where I have had to disclose it. While working at the insurance company I had scheduled doctors' appointments I couldn't miss after work, and it wasn't a problem. But at other jobs I've had a rotating schedule and employers have asked what the appointments were for. Being informed that it was a doctor's appointment, the employer would ask nothing further—but friends I worked with were curious. I also told those people I had insomnia and needed to meet with a doctor regularly for prescriptions.

For a while I was afraid people would learn I have schizoaffective and treat me differently and I did my best to hide it from others. Most people have no idea I have schizoaffective unless I tell them. My doctor assured me, "Fear not, the thing you are afraid of will most likely occur, but when it does it's nothing to be afraid of," quoting John McMurray. After finally realizing it was better to tell some close friends I had schizoaffective disorder than to hide it I learned he was exactly right. They did treat me differently initially and were overly kind and caring—and I was a bit perturbed—but there were no negative interactions and I wasn't disparaged for having a mental illness. They continued hanging out with me and eventually realized I am just like everyone else; after they became comfortable with knowing I had schizoaffective disorder, they went back to treating me the same way they did before.

One difficult facet of reintegrating in society is learning how to socialize. I spent at least four years in near isolation while psychotic, and had completely forgotten how to function socially, which left me fairly inept. I started by attending a group which consisted of people who also had mental illnesses and were in different phases of their recovery. Many were fully functional and understood that I was in a neurotic state of mind and needed help. Instead of ignoring me or shying away from me like people without mental illness would have, they interacted with me. Interacting with these people helped me to learn socialization skills; the more I attended the group the better I became at socializing. I made friends who had ailments similar to my own but were further along in their progress, so I was with healthy human beings who understood me and were willing to talk to me. Gaining exposure to socialization was one important facet of re-learning how to interact. I also talked about social norms and customs in therapy with my psychiatrist and used this group setting to practice implementing these socialization skills.

I also had some friends who work in mental health; when I informed them of my illness they were more willing to hang out with me. They knew I was a bit neurotic but still invited me to do things. This was another great way to spend time socializing with people who had an understanding of my predicament.

Another useful tool in helping me re-assimilate was watching television. During recovery, it was helpful because I was listening to socially adept people, some of whom were good conversationalists. I initially hated television but now I like it. Watching TV helped me identify social customs and norms I had previously forgotten. Listening to the sound of healthy voices, their way of speaking, and the subject matter they chose for conversation also helped improve my socialization skills.

After I became better at socializing with the people in my talk group, I began reintegrating with people who were not mentally ill. It was a rough transition and there were some awkward moments, but I thought of each interaction as a stepping stone and I learned a lot as I hung out with new groups of friends. I made friends with coworkers and I also joined a pool league where I met the friends I hang out with regularly. They knew I was a bit awkward but still hung out with me. As I spent more time with others I improved at socializing. I also spent a lot of time golfing with my Dad and his friends; doing so was great for my socialization skills because it was another situation where I was able to interact with fully functional people who were willing to be nice to me when I was awkward. The more I socialized the better I became at it. There were many awkward moments initially but I learned how to interact and the more I socialized the more I remembered about socializing. I currently have a vibrant social life and have different types of friends with whom I do different things. I have some friends who I'll just sit and talk with over coffee, while there are others who I'll golf or play sports with, and then there's some who I hang out with to have a lot of laughs.

I used to think that if something negative happened to me I must have deserved it, but this simply isn't true. Good things happen to bad people and bad things to good people. For a while I believed I deserved to lose my friends and I deserved all the negative consequences of my illness. I believed I was being justly punished for past wrongs and constantly thought I must have done something awful to deserve everything that had happened to me. This only created and perpetuated a negative self-perception. Most times there are consequences that directly correlate to a decision someone has made or to the way someone has decided to be, but other times occurrences happen at random. Someone could be living a very scrupulous life and then someone else might download a virus to his computer, causing him to lose his computing ability, which could cost a lot of time and energy. Someone else could be completely unscrupulous and win a scratch ticket for $20 million. Mental illness is an occurrence that happens at random. Also, in popular culture —in the movies and on television—there is almost always a correlation between the quality of someone's personality and the outcome of their situation, which corroborates the belief that if something bad has happened to a person, they must have done something to deserve it. Contrarily, no one decides to develop mental illness, it happens at random.

Sometimes it's difficult to identify the randomness of some occurrences in life because we so frequently correlate someone's state of being to his character or personality. People commonly try to draw connections between anything and everything, but I have learned to determine that sometimes things are not connected. Applying that lesson to my own experience with mental illness has been extremely helpful.

When I realized I didn't deserve mental illness it improved my self-esteem immensely and helped me to realize that my depression was a product of issues that occurred during episodes. There was no divine influence which examined the course of my life and determined that my actions merited mental illness. If there was a divine influence that examined my life before my illness, it would have determined that I didn't deserve to become mentally ill; I think most everyone can say the same thing. Having come to understand this, there were times when I still despairingly asked "Why me?" but I caught myself, realizing that if I despair, the illness will still exist, and negativity won't help resolve any of its issues. I realized I have to be positive and work towards optimizing my life regardless of the hand I've been dealt.

Becoming aware that I had not done anything prior to my development of schizoaffective disorder to cause its development was a great relief, because I had been constantly searching for reasons the illness occurred and had been blaming myself and constantly self-criticizing in an effort to discover the reason for it all.

Another difficult facet of mental illness is determining which behaviors are being caused by the illness and which ones are being caused by delusions. The illness-related issues are symptomatic, such as auditory hallucinations, a wider emotional range, and racing thoughts. However, there were many other psychological issues created by the episodes and by experiences that occurred outside of episodes which increased the intensity of my symptoms because they increased my stress levels. Those were things like losing my ability to socialize or to get along with others, or not being able to think with clarity or rationality. I addressed many issues regarding socialization and other things I could control, and eventually I regained skills I had lost, such as the ability to socialize well and think rationally. Overcoming adversities of this nature decreased my stress levels immensely because they yielded great benefits. Having friends was something I was extremely grateful for; being able to think with clarity, rationality, and logic helped me in a myriad of ways. As my stress decreased so did the intensity and frequency of my symptoms, such as referential thinking, auditory hallucinations, and paranoia. Talking about stressful experiences which were still unsettled in my psyche helped to almost eliminate these symptoms. I have not experienced referential thinking for at least a couple years and I've experienced very few auditory hallucinations.

During episodes, my illness caused me to believe many delusions and develop some strange habits, and after the episodes those thoughts and behaviors still existed. There were also other consequences of episodes, such as losing all my friends, becoming morbidly depressed from overmedication, and being unable to function socially because I didn't understand how to carry on conversations, having been estranged and alone for so long. My episodes changed my psychology and I needed talk therapy to work through those issues. Many of the symptoms were partially alleviated from medication but many remained because they were psychological. Knowing this allowed me to take a great step forward. I understood that all the psychological problems which resulted from the illness are solvable through talk therapy and journaling because they are issues which were created by an impetus, the illness, which is no longer present. It took time and courage for me to eliminate the issues which were caused by the illness but only perpetuated by my remembrance of traumatic experiences and the meaning I had assigned to them.

Understanding I am not my illness has been extremely beneficial because it informs me that I am as functional as anyone else and that am just as human. I know my illness only affects my ability to rationally process and filter information while I am experiencing an episode, but otherwise does not have any influence in my life. I don't consider myself someone who has deficiencies while healthy, though I am still aware that—because there is an illness—there is always the potential for symptoms to occur. I understand that I am different from other people—but most everyone is different, regardless of how much people prefer to believe they are exactly the same. I also know I can function just as well as everyone else and achieve just as much if not more than everyone else despite my mental illness.

There are also direct correlations between thoughts within my mind and symptoms of bipolarity. I do have a wider emotional range than others but the way my emotions are expressed is determined by my way of thinking, the way I am living, and/or the experiences lodged in my memory. The sleeplessness and wider emotional range were a direct result of the illness and they contributed to my anger but there were psychological burdens that were the main factors in my mercurial moods. My extreme anger during my second episode was mostly a result of sleeplessness coupled with many unaddressed psychological issues. I later addressed these experiences and gained a better understanding of them. Understanding the reasons my life had been so difficult during my earlier years eliminated a lot of my anger for a number of reasons. Most of my bipolarity was a result of having experienced such a difficult life and then seeing elements of that experience creep back into the present. Once I figured out who I wanted to be and how to stand up for myself, my mood seemed to level out. I also came to realize that the main reason I was ostracized while younger was my inability to functionally interact socially. This only occurred because of my cognitive impairment and lack of education; I realized that with the medication and my work on improving my socialization skills, I wouldn't have to worry about being socially inept or inarticulate. People would no longer assume that I must be unintelligent and ostracize me. I have also addressed other issues that created anger for me, and I have had little, if any, anger for the past three to four years. Friends of mine joke about a time when I was angry during a bad round of golf, because it was so out of the ordinary for them to have witnessed any expression of anger at all from me.

I searched for new music which had a positive, uplifting mood and I found some guitar music without lyrics which met this criterion. I bought many songs and listened to the new music during my daily commute. After a couple weeks, I noticed a change in my emotions and realized it was because of the music. Every occurrence in our lives is retained somewhere within our memories. The practice of remembering is reconnecting to these particular files in the brain. Recent memories have a stronger effect on the psyche in the present, which is why listening to positive music helped me keep a positive attitude. Part of me still felt a need to listen to negative and melancholy music, but only out of habit. Habit creates comfort and comfort is enjoyable. I had been gaining comfort from the habit of listening to negative and melancholy music. It wasn't from the messages or moods that were being expressed. There is a Harvard Research Study that proves this. The practice of assigning a positive meaning to negative music had also caused me to affiliate positive emotions with negative ideas. This created ambivalence and confusion in my thinking. After eliminating the convolution of connecting negative ideas with positive emotions, my thinking became more lucid because my emotions were matched up with with the reality of the ideas.

Although music and reading improved my mood, at the age of 25 I was still in somewhat of a depression from my psychological disposition and from medication.

I was sleeping ten hours a night and had trouble finding motivation to do things I enjoyed. I was in a funk and was searching for ways to snap out of it, but regardless of what I tried I felt strapped down. Being depressed feels as though someone is holding your emotions in a straight jacket and regardless of what you do, you can't release yourself from it. We tried some anti-depressants but the lightest doses were too strong and I was experiencing side-effects that were worse than being depressed.

I eventually realized I felt energized on days I drank coffee, so I began drinking one cup every morning. The small boost from the coffee helped lift the depression and I felt energized. I still drink one cup of coffee each morning and take medication at night. There were still issues in my life I needed to address, but the coffee was definitely helpful.

For three years, I stuck with 2 mg Risperidone and was still symptomatic. Many of my symptoms were a result of psychological trauma but I was still able to find a good amount of relief from medication. I was extremely stubborn when asked if I would like to increase my medication even the slightest amount because of my previous experience of having been overmedicated. However, I thought about increasing the medication and my doctor and I figured if I dislike it I can always revert to the previous dose. I increased my Risperidone intake to 3 mg instead of 2, which was extremely helpful. The increase improved my stream of consciousness, helped reduce referential thinking, and most importantly reduced my paranoia. I also eventually decided to take Clonozapam, an anti-anxiety medication, which helped limit social anxiety.

I have my pharmacy's phone number programmed into my cell phone to save time while calling in prescriptions. I also have my psychiatrist's number programmed into my phone in case I am running late or need to call for any other reasons. Prescriptions usually contain 30 pills and are only refillable 28 days after submission because I am prescribed to take 1 pill per day and they want to prevent anyone from obtaining a surplus of medication. My doctor prescribed backup medication which I can take in case I run out of my original prescription and am unable to refill it. I take 3mg of Risperdone so my doctor prescribed a bottle of 1mg Risperdone pills for backup. If I am feeling symptomatic I can also take an extra 1mg pill to help but usually find it unnecessary. Prescriptions are usually accompanied with 3 refills and once these are exhausted patients are required to obtain a new script to get more medication. There are many reasons why I might be unable to request a new script and pick it up in time, such as going out of town or having the prescription run out at the start of a holiday. If you can't get backup medication for these times the pharmacy will usually give you several days worth of medication, provided they can find you in the system and have preciously filled prescriptions for the medication you are requesting. I also keep some medication in my car's glove compartment, so I have the option of sleeping over at friends' houses instead of having to leave while I am still awake enough to drive home to take my medication. I know my medication takes an hour to take effect; I take it one hour before I want to sleep and it has worked every night. I haven't missed one night's rest since I began taking it, which has been an extraordinary benefit.

One night while I had a cold I took over-the-counter medication with an antihistamine and woke up extremely dizzy the next morning. I called the pharmacy and they informed me my medication doesn't mix well with antihistamines and that I should avoid taking antihistamines for colds. I have a friend who called his pharmacy and they informed him it would be all right to mix Risperdone with an over the counter antihistamine. They told him he would only feel a little dizzy, but when he awoke he experienced psychotic symptoms. It's important to check with reliable sources before mixing any medications.

Living in the present is important because it is the only time someone can implement agency and change and influence their life in a positive manner. It is also the only time anyone ever experiences thoughts, feelings, emotions and everything else happening in life. For a while I was depressed and felt awful about my life and wanted to avoid living in the present because of depression. I tried thinking of other times to take my mind off my current circumstances, rather than thinking of how I could change my life and make it better. I eventually realized that if I wanted anything to change I needed to face the problems which existed in the present. I worked through them and have had everything to gain for it.

Acclimating one's mind to the present is accomplished by staying active. Activities require one to think in the present and make decisions. Active people are far better at creating change and making a difference in their lives while those who remain passive sometimes spend their lives waiting for things to change. Things rarely change on their own.

A cultivated mind is able to implement agency far better than an uncultivated mind. Engaging my mind by reading, playing brain games, and thinking about life helped me improve intellectually. I had always read a little, but at about age 25 I began reading more frequently and improving my intellect. As I have improved my intelligence, living with mental illness has become far easier because I can implement my knowledge to my advantage. As my intelligence has increased and my mind's functionality has improved, I have been able to develop a better stream of consciousness, improve my memory, and cultivate many other tools which I have been able to use to overcome schizoaffective disorder.

I've talked to people with mental illness who like mental illness related literature and entertainment and to others who don't. Mel Gibson's character in *Conspiracy Theory* disconcerts me because he accurately depicts a demeanor which is similar to mine while I am ill; I changed the channel a few minutes in. I also had difficulty watching *A Beautiful Mind.* I thought it would be educational but I was fairly depressed for two hours after the movie.

Reading has been incredibly important for me. For one thing, it has improved my memory. Long term memory is essential for remembering past experiences but short term and active memory is even more useful, because it helps us retain thoughts while developing other thoughts. The ability to keep thoughts in mind allows us to consider ideas and concepts at length and examine them on deeper levels, thus enabling us to learn more. Reading also develops the stream of consciousness and solidifies word-concept relations. Many times, people know a concept but don't have the word for it; they are unable to think lucidly about it because they simply can't name it. Too many words are required to talk about a concept that can't be named, and the thoughts surrounding the concept become muddled and nebulous. When our vocabulary makes it possible to identify concepts, they can be pondered and ruminated over, which is an important practice in problem solving and creative thinking. Verbalizing thoughts is useful for creating change in life, because when a goal is clearly verbalized it provides a clear and accurate focal point for the goal and enables us to hone in on it and reach it faster.

Reading also awakens the mind and develops awareness. During and after my recovery from schizoaffective disorder I used auto-bibliotherapy along with talk therapy to improve the quality of my life. Having a cognitive impairment during my earlier years left me poorly equipped in matters of wisdom and I didn't think with any particular depth about life. I started doing so once I became an English major and later realized literature had many useful lessons that could help me overcome mental illness and also many that would just make me a better person. A great deal of the issues I had were normal life issues and I gained a better understanding of my life just by reading fiction and philosophy. I've used many lessons learned from literature and philosophy to answer questions that were related to mental illness.

When I began delving into my self-psychoanalysis in my notebook I read existentialism and psychology to gain a better understanding of life. My doctor recommended *Man's Search for Meaning* by Victor Frankl. I think this book is a must read for everyone. I learned about logos therapy, which is a therapy where we change the meaning surrounding situations, thus changing our perception of the situations and empowering ourselves. Through logos therapy I came to see myself as someone who would overcome mental illness and any other burdens in my life and live as happily as I could rather than being burdened by anything.

While in the victim mind set, I was depressed and overwhelmed and floundered to gain a foothold in life. I remember being in a psychology class during my first episode. A young adult with downs syndrome was interviewed. He expressed his disappointment at not being able to express his thoughts as well as everyone else, and he was crying. I too started crying because this resonated so strongly with my own experience.

I eventually realized that overcoming mental illness and any other adversity is an opportunity for achievement that holds a great deal of meaning. The goal is to never allow mental illness or any other burden to hinder the quality of my life or prevent me from doing anything anyone else can do; to enjoy life as much as possible. Changing my perception of mental illness enhanced and completely transformed the quality of my life. It motivated me to persist while facing tough adversity because it provided a meaning for enduring the illness and its aftermath. In short, I find happiness to be an extraordinary *achievement*. What was once burdensome has now become an opportunity for success and provides my life with meaning. Having a meaningful life is fulfilling because it has made my life feel purposeful and worth while.

My change of perception has motivated me to attack any adversity I'm facing and to overcome it, regardless of whether or not it is related to mental illness. I've used the resources and strength I've gained from having to face mental illness in other situations, which has made situations that were previously difficult become incredibly easy.

It's important to note I don't seek out adversity to overcome it. However, when I'm faced with adversity, I use logos therapy for support.

Even if mental illness is diminishing the quality of my life in some way or for some period of time, I find meaning in my will to endure and in my will to continue working towards resolutions for the problems it's causing. I see endurance and the effort to problem-solve as achievements in themselves because, although I am burdened, I haven't capitulated. So even while mental illness or other circumstances may be having a negative effect on me, I have still created a positive situation just by refusing to be defeated.

There have been times where I have felt I was facing adversity on all fronts and was nearly overwhelmed. Everywhere I turned there seemed to be something going wrong and life was extremely tough. I still occasionally have days like that. The way I cope is to start with the most important issue I can think of and go to work in talk therapy and journaling. Yes, it is stressful to feel overwhelmed, but it gets me motivated and fired up to think "The kitchen sink has been thrown at me, but I'm going to pick it all up and throw it right back!"

Although facing adversity can be meaningful this meaning doesn't always eliminate the detriments of the situation and all its burdens. Sometimes there are things we simply just have to do. Sometimes the things that are right and best for us can be the most difficult things to do, but this is another situation where I've used logos therapy to change the meaning surrounding a situation to motivate myself to persist. In psychotherapy, I've had to come to terms with, analyze, and resolve issues that I was afraid of and made me very uneasy. I eventually realized it was for the best to face my fears and I decided to "see the benefits I would gain from actions I had to carry out" (Nietzsche) rather than thinking about the detriments of the situation. I was forced to relive traumatizing moments and re-experience the emotions of those situations during therapy. By simply changing my perception of a situation from something I had to endure and battle with to something that could provide me extraordinary benefits, I gained the courage I needed to face these fears. I knew by enduring the remembrance of my most traumatizing experiences, which was extremely difficult, I would eventually alleviate the anxieties caused by them, so I did. I now enjoy recognizing my insecurities, because I know I can find alleviation for them. For instance, for a good portion of my life I hardly ever expressed my true thoughts, always trying to "go along" with the group. That was because of my fear of estrangement. I have recognized that fear and addressed it; I am now an individual and simply do what I think is best, regardless of who is or isn't doing it, and feel fine spending time alone.

I sometimes wondered, "How does my life make a difference?" Ultimately, I concluded that if it doesn't make a difference to anyone else it still makes a difference to me, and I still want it to be as good as it can be because I'm the one experiencing it. I wondered if I was important and realized that I am. I make a difference to myself and the people in my life.

After I published my first article, titled "The Importance of Talk Therapy," in Schizophrenia Bulletin, I shared it with a friend who is a poet and has taught me a lot about writing. He said one of the best things about the article was the gratitude I expressed for being able to recover from schizoaffective disorder and for having had people in my life who were helpful. Gratitude was a concept I had never connected with mental illness, and it made me wonder what I have to be grateful for. I've always felt I would never wish this experience upon anyone, because I've been forced to face years of extreme adversity. I eventually realized that dealing with this illness has helped me develop strength, character, intelligence, and resources I would have never acquired had I never had the illness. My experiences have transformed my life, and although I was put on an extremely difficult path, I worked through it and I am happy being the person I am today.

Schizoaffective disorder took tenacity to overcome. Even now there are still issues I am working through, but but I intend to iron them out. I was incapacitated to the point where I was estranged from my family and friends, unable to think a coherent thought or speak an understandable sentence, or work any type of job. Once I decided I wanted a better life and put forth the effort to improve my life I began progressing. There were times when I struggled but I persisted and my life changed because of my willingness to work. I realized I have agency and can implement change and this realization encouraged me to make healthy decisions and to work hard in therapy. Talk therapy and journaling are the medicines that changed my life. They rehabilitated me to the point where I now hold a full-time job and have a vibrant social life where I am going out three to four times a week; I participate in a writing group, I am a published writer, and I'm dating. Most importantly, I have reconnected with my family and I have some great friends.

In recent months, I've revealed to several people that I know very well the fact that I have schizoaffective disorder, and they've all responded that they never would have known it had I not said anything. The most useful knowledge for overcoming mental illness and its aftermath was believing I had the ability to do so and having faith that I could continually improve and eventually get to where I wanted to be. These beliefs coupled with a strong work ethic helped me become a far better person than I ever would have been had the illness never developed.

Postscript
Symptoms and Solutions

Suicide Prevention and Self-Esteem

About a year and a half after my first episode of schizoaffective disorder I was still severely depressed. Mustering enough energy to make it through the day was extremely difficult. I had just begun working for an insurance company in customer service and my life was beginning to improve but I still didn't have any of the things I wanted. My life lacked meaning; just making it from one day to the next was a struggle. Some days I thought if I had an easy way to commit suicide—such as using a gun—I would probably do it. I even went as far as briefly fathoming how to get a gun. The main reasons I had suicidal thoughts were lacking meaning in life, lacking the things I wanted out of life, and being burdened by poor self-esteem from having experienced two episodes in the past five years and extreme depressions in their aftermath.

My mom knew I wasn't religious but also knew I still believed in morality. She mentioned conversationally that suicide is a sin and this resonated strongly with me. I thought if I committed suicide my last act would be sinful and I would go to hell forever, which I didn't want. I currently am not religious but this idea still resonates strongly with me. This was one preventative measure that helped keep me alive. Even so, I was still extremely depressed. My negative emotions were a heavy cloak that was suffocating me and it held fast for quite some time.

When I thought about suicide and felt I couldn't live for myself I did my best to live for the few people in my life who I felt cared for me. I sometimes pictured how difficult it would be for my parents and sister to go on without me, and this also helped keep me around. Eventually the thought of my family missing me didn't matter that much in my mind, so I searched for someone else to live for. I wanted to make a difference in the world in some way; I had a decent pay check so I decided I would sponsor a child in Africa. I chose this child because I knew he had been starving and lacked many basic necessities and was living in a manner that was somewhat similar to my predicament during my first episode. I knew what it was like to starve and lack basic needs so it made me feel good to know I was relieving someone of a burden that I had personally experienced and had known to be horrible. I still sponsor him to this day. I picked a reputable company and sent thirty dollars per month and my donations boosted my self-esteem substantially. Some days when I had suicidal thoughts I felt I had to continue on so I could help my sponsored child live a good life. The feeling that I had to live to help someone else live improved my self-perception. It started making me feel that I was worth while because I felt useful to someone. I still had a great deal of issues from my episodes and their aftermath but the sponsorship of the child gave me a reason to persist.

From this experience I learned that I love helping other people. I looked for work outside of the insurance company and considered teaching and writing. I eventually decided against teaching but still knew that writing was a great way to help others and began developing my craft. Everyone I talked to about writing was really encouraging; this was important because writing meant more to me at that time than anyone I was talking to ever knew. I considered myself someone who was supported by a three-legged stool because if any leg of the stool broke—if I could not afford to help the African child, if learning writing was out of my reach—I probably would have fallen hard to the ground and into another depression. The dream of becoming a writer made me very hopeful that I could help a lot of people and I knew that helping others made me feel worth while. I was still in a precarious state of mind when I began to pursue writing. Luckily, I decided I would start my writing career by creating a memoir. After writing about seventy to ninety pages of this memoir I determined that I still wasn't at a point in my life where I was happy with the way things were going.

I realized I had to start helping myself if I wanted to help anyone else. This began a three-year period where I basically transformed my mind and life through metacognition, talk therapy, journaling, and many other forms of therapy. I began attacking all the issues that had been hampering me. Tackling issue after issue, I progressed into better states of being. I worked to improve every day and learned new things about myself constantly. Sometimes there were goals that seemed way out of reach—like being able to make friends. Rather than despair, I chose to look at the progress I had already made with socializing and remembered situations where I did well socially. I used my past successes to boost my confidence. There were many times when I had difficulty envisioning my life beyond its current state, so I simply worked on the things that were more immediate through talk therapy and journaling. I told myself, "If I was able to make it as far as I already have, then I can keep on going, and at some point, I'll have what I want out of life." I developed a lot of hope from looking back and noting the improvements and differences between my previous state of being and my current one. This motivated me to keep working and keep improving as much as I could. I now live a life where I feel I am walking on an endless horizon. The thought that I can keep advancing my life beyond its current state means a great deal to me.

I used to think that, if I didn't have friends, a meaningful job, a girlfriend, fun activities to participate in and all the other things I wanted, I must not be deserving of a good life. I thought must be a lack of character that prevented me from obtaining these things. Finally, I realized that three years of schizoaffective disorder had jolted me off the tracks and thrown me into an extremely difficult position. Through my work in self-improvement I learned increasingly more about my life and life in general, and I was finally able to dispel the issues that had been hampering my self-esteem. I realized I hadn't intentionally done anything to make myself into someone who was unable to functionally interact with others, or have a job I liked, or have all the things I wanted out of life. I was finally able to see that I was a good person myself; my sole purpose for living didn't need to be supporting and helping other people, (although I still enjoy doing so). Eventually, I figured out the reason I was depressed. It was simply not having the things I wanted out of life and not being healthy enough to get those things or having any hope I would ever obtain them. This realization was extremely liberating, because I was no longer blaming myself for the adverse emotions and situations I had been experiencing while trying to regain my mental health and reconstruct my life. I learned it was not my fault at all; ridding myself of the blame for my illness boosted my self-esteem immensely. I no longer held myself accountable for having lost all my friends, or having been basically homeless, and all the other aforementioned miseries I experienced. It finally gave me the feeling that I do in fact deserve to have a great life. Having the hope that I could obtain the things I wanted out of life motivated me to do everything I could to provide myself with a great life. This created an inclination for progress.

I currently have a number of family members,

friends, and other supportive people who count on me and who I know I can count on. I also have a number of activities I participate in such as writing, working, shooting pool, golfing, hanging out with friends, and a number of other things I enjoy doing to support me and keep me occupied. I currently have most of the things I want in life, haven't had a suicidal thought for at least two years, and consider myself a happy person. I am continuing to work towards improving the quality of my life and the functionality of my mind while helping others do the same.

Obsessive Behaviors and Exposure Therapy

During both my schizoaffective disorder episodes, I had many obsessive behaviors which were detrimental to my health. I set about cleaning everything and anything I owned as well as I possibly could. I once emptied my room and cleaned every single thing I owned top to bottom, including the room. I scrubbed the ceilings three times over, washed the walls and windows, and hired a carpet cleaner to professionally clean the carpet—twice. I cleaned my hands so repetitively and thoroughly that they had tons of little cuts on them and looked as though I had run them through buckets of glass shards. I had become a germaphobe because I thought external purity created internal purity. I believed I was a messiah and if I was to save the world I needed to be pure.

Overcoming my abnormal fear of germs took mental flexibility, which I worked on with my doctor in talk therapy. We searched for reasons why I had an abnormal fear and I eventually disclosed how I thought I would become a messiah if I did everything correctly and was a pure person. A couple of years after I had stopped obsessively hand washing, I uncovered the deeper reasons for the hand washing, which came down to wanting more control over my life. Being in a schizoaffective disorder episode is very disorienting and precarious. I felt if I had control over my material possessions and they were clean, my mind would be cleaner; I would be able to think more clearly and have more mental control.

It took time to face the fears that generated the hand washing, and even after I had determined the reasons for my excessive washing I was still afraid to refrain from doing so. I understood the surface logic of the argument against over-washing, but I wouldn't listen because I had emotional connections and irrational subconscious fears connected to my obsessive habits. At that time, I wasn't able to delve deep enough into my mind to understand the way I was thinking while obsessive compulsions were occurring.

Although I didn't know the deepest reasons I obsessively washed, having some basic logic to understand my habit helped me move towards exposing myself to not washing my hands. Many times when I've had an irrational fear, I've found dozens of questions or doubts opposing a change of habit and have had to answer those questions and refute those doubts before having the courage to face and eliminate the fear. While facing the compulsive hand washing I worried, "Is not washing my hands and then coming in contact with others disrespectful?" and "Will my health diminish if I don't wash my hands as thoroughly and frequently as I have been?" Talk therapy and journaling have been extremely helpful in eliminating questions and doubts of this nature. In the earlier stages of my recovery I almost always needed talk therapy and the guidance of my doctor to help refute these questions, but as my mental health and intelligence have improved, I've been able to more frequently eliminate these questions by journaling. When I have been able to better understand the reasons why I am afraid of an experience, it has given me more courage to face my fear.

At this point my hands were cut and in pain and I knew I wasn't a messiah anymore but still washed them. My doctor recommended exposure therapy where I exposed myself to not washing them and had to deal with the emotions of the experience first hand. My anxiety was extremely high after the first couple times of not washing them excessively. I had compulsions to return to washing them but kept disciplined and avoided it. Watching myself overcome my fear in the context of my own life was extremely helpful. Now I had empirical knowledge to corroborate the ideas my doctor was impressing upon me; this first-hand experience stood up to any questions I could pose; it simply held true. I experienced the thing I was afraid of and gradually began feeling safer.

Although I knew I was all right after refraining from excessive washing, there was always a nagging urge to go back and wash because I still felt anxiety. But I fought it. There were times when not washing my hands excessively felt terrifying, but I realized the anxiety was coming from other issues in my life and not from any real need to wash my hands. This knowledge helped me completely dismiss my delusion. Once I realized that the anxiety had its source in other issues, any urge to excessively wash was completely eliminated.

As I moved away from my episode and became healthier I still wanted clean hands but also had a more rational mind. I decided for some instances I would just use water and for others I would use soap and water. When it comes to obsessive behaviors, I simply have to identify what the purpose of the behavior is and fulfill that purpose, then move on to a different task. Of course, I now understand I am not a messiah and don't need to purify myself at all. Even so, I have put a safeguard in place against the obsessive cleaning. I've told myself a certain amount of dirt has to remain on the earth; we don't want to exhaust our natural resources while excessively cleaning everything. I am currently aware that I can miss a hand washing with no negative repercussions, and am fairly certain the world isn't going to run out of resources because of cleaning—but I know I think differently during episodes. I don't think OCD will ever be a problem for me again but I've put safeguards of this nature in place in case of another episode.

When I'm facing new fears and preparing to be exposed to them, I remember previous times when I was exposed to something that frightened me, which had a positive outcome. I remind myself that I felt no negative repercussions. Doing this has given me the courage to face t new fears and undergo exposure therapy. Sometimes these positive memories have completely eliminated the fear altogether, and I've felt no anxiety or any negative emotions while facing the experience I was afraid of.

Understanding Referential and Metaphoric Thinking

I developed referential thinking where I thought people were directly referencing me in conversation when in fact they were only talking about the subject they had mentioned. Someone could be saying, "I hate that, it's really awful," and I would think they were indirectly saying they hated me and that I was awful. My referential thinking usually occurred while I was feeling stressed and had poor self-esteem. I believed I was an unlikeable person, which made me feel others would think the same thing and want to mention it. When people used pronouns, I often substituted myself for the pronoun, even if the person wasn't talking about me. For example, a person might say, "*Someone* took too many cookies." They could have been talking about my sister, but I would perceive them as talking about me. When I knew exactly who or what the speaker was talking about, I was less likely to substitute my name for the pronoun. The people expressing negativity were simply disappointed about the subject they were discussing. I only assumed that the subject of their statement was in some way intended to be me, and the descriptions referencing the subject were intended to describe me. I've had to remind myself that a speaker is only talking about the subject he's actually mentioned; that subject is not a symbol which is intended to indicate me. That way I can determine who or what the speaker is actually talking about and realize his words have nothing to do with me.

Some of the referential thinking occurred when I returned to environments similar to those I had been in during episodes, such as a school setting. I returned to school for graduate courses and during my first couple days experienced a great deal of referential thinking. Being in a college setting triggered the same emotions I felt during my first episode because much of it was spent in class. The combination of the classroom environment and the same emotions I'd experienced during episodes made me feel I was in the same situation again. My thinking also became somewhat disoriented as a result of feeling paranoia, which I had also experienced during my first episode. Once I was able to tell myself this situation was completely different than what I'd gone through during my episodes, the referential thinking subsided and I was able to function and interact. I realized that, when I'm in situations similar to those I'd been in during episodes, I am more susceptible to experiencing schizoaffective symptoms. Referential thinking has also had a direct correlation to my stress levels. I know when I am feeling stressed it can be more likely to occur. Knowing these things has allowed me to anticipate when referential thinking might occur. When I have expected referential thinking to occur, I've reminded myself I need to connect the statement the speaker is making directly to the subject matter they are talking about.

There are times where people simply want to vent a negative thought and I just happen to be the person they decide to speak to. Usually, when people want to say something about someone they are with, they'll either address that person directly. They either make it very obvious they are referencing a particular person and ensure that person knows they are being referenced, or they don't express their feelings about that person at all. People who approached me with negativity and anger confused me; I felt I had done something to make them angry. Sometimes people are just in bad moods and the cause is independent of everyone around them, including myself. Something may be happening in their life which has them thinking negatively, and they'll still be angry regardless of how they are approached or who they are talking to.

Another way to eliminate referential thinking is by evaluating situations from an objective standpoint. When I have sought to understand the true reasons people are angry while talking to me, I have realized sometimes people are in bad moods, some people are just angry about something in their life. I have also realized I didn't say or do anything which created their anger, which makes me independent of their statements. Sometimes I realize the person was in a negative mood before I was talking to them, which is why the first thing they said to me was something negative. Other times I realize that people sometimes completely switch subjects in conversation and their switch to something negative was simply their own doing, independent of anything I said or did.

Another facet of referential thinking is interpreting people's body language and tone. Often when people are relating a negative thought they'll look angry and it may seem as though they are angry at me, but in reality, they were only relating their emotions through facial expressions and body language. People who are speaking angrily or negatively about something are outwardly expressing these emotions while speaking about the impetus for these emotions, and may seem to be directing this anger towards their listener while doing so. This happens even when they are angry at something other than their listener—who may happen to be me. This can be confusing, because they are directing anger stemming from something else apparently towards me, merely because I am the one listening, not because they actually have any anger at me, or because of me.

There were times where it seemed as though people were looking at me hatefully, in reproach, but this illusion was self-perpetuated. The person would begin conveying a negative thought; I believed he was speaking in reference to me. That would trigger negative and shameful body language from me, which would cause the speaker to look at me reproachfully. The only reason he looked at me reproachfully was my body language. In reality the person speaking held no grudge against me; most times we were only barely acquainted; he knew nothing about me. But people may think that if there is reason for me to be ashamed, which shows in my demeanor and body language, then there is reason for them to reproach me. The speaker acted on the emotional cue I was creating.

The same concept is applicable to most emotions.

Metaphoric thinking was another problem I had, which resulted partially from reading a lot of fiction. Fiction is heavily imbued with metaphor; and the more I have read the easier I have been able to perceive metaphor in everyday life. During episodes, I thought everything happening in my life was metaphor and was happening because some force wanted to inform me more about my life and my future. I have learned to first discern reality from fiction, so when I am not reading I realize this is real life and the occurrences happening are completely disconnected from one another. Understanding exactly what metaphor is has helped me eliminate metaphoric thinking. In literary works, a metaphor is a word or phrase that carries more than one meaning. The first denotes something that exists in the actual world. That thing has characteristics which are like those of some other thing, real or imagined. The metaphor makes a connection between the two things, pointing to an abstract meaning they seem to share, which comprises the essence of the comparison

Metaphor is a literary device. In the real world, though people may occasionally use metaphors, like "it's raining cats and dogs," they do not generally speak metaphorically; they do not speak of one thing in terms of another, they just say what they mean, and there is no "deeper meaning" implied. When I was able to realize this, it helped me to refute the connections I had been perceiving that didn't actually exist.

I'll give you an example of how metaphorical thinking confused me. If someone said, "He's ascending the steps," his meaning should be obvious: someone is walking up a flight of stairs. But to that meaning I would add a "deeper meaning" that applied to me; I would perceive the sentence to mean that I was moving up in life, spiritually. The abstract connection would be *ascendance*.

Coincidences happen, but people usually aren't creating these metaphoric demonstrations to provide me with information.

I thought these metaphors were occurring as a result of divinity sending me messages, but I have realized there is no divinity sending me messages in any way whatsoever, never mind metaphorically. At one point, if a virus had been downloaded to my computer, I might have perceived that as a divine message, telling myself, "Yes, I do have a virus on my computer, but also a virus in my brain—that being mental illness, which to me correlated metaphorically. I have learned to separate the context of the two situations by stating that my brain is separate from my computer and this virus is different from my mental illness. This is an example of an occurrence where coincidentally two things could seem connected but are really separate.

Language and Recovery

During my schizoaffective episodes, speaking and understanding what what said to me in conversation was very difficult for me, despite my being an English major (I even completed all my course work and passed most of my classes during my first episode). The most difficult part of schizoaffective disorder for me was my inability to effectively communicate with others. Although I was unable to clearly express my thoughts I still had clear thoughts; in fact, I was constantly thinking, as I believe most people are during their episodes. I spent days without saying more than several words to several people, and that got me too much inside my own mind. Spending so much time thinking alone by myself started creating problems, such as referential and metaphoric thinking. The most confusing part of schizophrenia was the inability to discern the internal from the external; it did not help that I spent so much time inside my own mind driving my internal monologue. Worse than living on the floor of an apartment with very little heat in the middle of a New England winter and nearly starving was the loneliness I felt. My inability to communicate and converse created this loneliness. I constantly dreamed of being lauded by millions of people after having saved the world (because I thought I was the next messiah), but the point is, if I had more help with my socialization I would have overcome my illness much faster.

In the years following my episodes I still struggled to find happiness, largely because of my inability to socialize effectively. Achieving life goals was the most essential part of therapy for me because it created the most happiness, and most of my life goals revolved around socializing, such as having friends to hang out with, having a job, having a girlfriend, and having a meaningful life. If I had spent more time working on my communication and socialization skills I would have achieved my life goals much faster. The development of my ability to understand and create language has been essential to my recovery and to my advance beyond recovery.

During my episodes, I intentionally isolated myself from society to figure out my life. I became so trapped inside myself as a result of insomnia, schizoaffective disorder, and poor dietary habits that I had a great deal of difficulty discerning the internal from the external. Although I was in a bad state of mind I was still able to communicate with others, but my conversations were very tumultuous. I had created a series of rules that I thought everyone needed to abide by while talking to me; otherwise I wouldn't say anything to them. One rule was that no one should ever tell me—or even suggest for me—what I ought to do. During and shortly after my episodes, I did not respond well to commands under any conditions. I wanted to do what was best but didn't want to be told to do it. Sometimes my parents would command me to do things and I simply wouldn't listen, because I was sick of being told what to do. I would tell myself in my mind, "No, I won't do that" and then do it anyways. A lot of the time I was willing to do whatever anyone *asked* me to do so long as they asked me in an objective and non-assuming tone.

At the time, I wanted to become an independent thinker and thought a lot of the problems I had encountered in my earlier life were the result of listening too much to others. There were times where people would suggest what I ought to do, for any number of reasons, and I would know they were correct but I still claimed to disagree with them. By outwardly disagreeing with what they were telling me, I could assert my independence and then make the decision for myself; then I would usually do exactly the thing they recommended. Asking me open-ended questions in an objective tone usually got the best results from me. Being open ended means none of the possible answers were inserted into the question; therefore, I would have to come up with a course of action on my own—which is exactly what I wanted to do at that time, all the time. The objective tone was important, because I sometimes assumed if someone made the correct answer sound obvious, it

was a means of persuading me. I hated persuasiveness. If I picked up on any persuasiveness during my
episodes I usually started arguing. I also hated manipu-
lation. Although my mind wasn't functioning as well as
everyone else's, I still knew when people were being
manipulative. It disinclined me to listen to them and
gave me motivation to do the opposite of what they intended. However, when people were up front with me
and open about their intentions and their desires, I was
far more willing to listen and comply. I had more respect
for people who were up front with me and I trusted
them more; I was more willing to listen to them, and got
along better with them. The only people I really talked
to during episodes were my parents and my teachers.
The teachers were the ones I listened to.

In earlier years, I had felt my life was meaningless and during my episodes I was doing everything
possible to ensure that my life was meaningful. -

I hated sarcasm, and never used it, because I
thought it would condition my mind to say the opposite
of what I thought. I now understand that the tone assigned to sarcasm actually indicates that the thought
being stated is ridiculous, but I also didn't understand
that at the time. I didn't think my mind could factor in
tone of voice as having meaning. I didn't want to tell
myself to do the opposite of what I wanted to do, because I thought it would create a lot of problems. I became annoyed and didn't talk much to people who were
sarcastic, who said what they didn't mean instead of
saying exactly what they meant. I think I would have
been more willing to talk to others if they had stated exactly what they meant instead of stating what they didn't
mean. I still prefer to simply say what I mean, the reason being that I can more accurately pinpoint my
thoughts and understand what things are, instead of
having an idea of what they are not. During my

episodes I knew I had difficulty with language, and this was one way I was working to get a better grasp on using language to accurately describe things in my life.

Another thing that made communication difficult for me was ambiguity. I found that when people created shorter but complete sentences— with a clear subject and verb— I was better able to understand them. It was difficult to understand people when they made vague references. A vague reference is a statement such as "It goes over there". If someone stated "The lamp goes on the table," I would have been able to better understand them. The difference between these two sentences is that the latter uses nouns rather than pronouns. This is important for two reasons. One is that my language processing ability was diminished and my intuition was weaker while I was feeling ill, so I was less able to figure out what people meant when they used vague references. The use of nouns was more helpful simply for my language comprehension. Another reason was because I was more prone to referential thinking when I heard a pronoun than when I heard a noun. When I was not feeling well I was putting myself in place of the subject of the sentence and interpreting the sentence as having something to do with my own life. When the subject of sentence was clearly stated, I was less likely to mistake the sentence as referring to myself, imagining that it contained some sort of deeper meaning relating to my life, or offered me some sort of instruction as to what I ought to be doing.

After my episodes I was less paranoid but still had many issues I had to address and my socialization skills were being hampered by them. I had spent about two years in poor mental health with a great amount of psychosis. As a result, I had completely forgotten how to socialize and did not know what was socially acceptable or how to really connect to anyone. I still thought I was a messiah and did not want to ingest any material that had any bad influences in it, such as violent TV shows or radio songs full of negativity. Since I didn't want to listen to the radio or watch most TV shows, I wasn't getting much opportunity to listen to anyone speaking. Reading was helpful for me, but to effectively interact with others I needed to speak and listen to people more. Eventually I found artists who had positive messages and uplifting music and also found programs that were worth watching. Hearing the voices of people who were mentally healthy and rational—and who were good conversationalists—was immensely beneficial for my socialization skills. I watched mostly sports and classics made into movies and I listened to NPR radio, and The Beatles. Listening to these voices gave me a sense of how to interact with others and a sense of what was socially acceptable and not acceptable.

Although I was improving I was still having difficulty socializing because of issues from my childhood and from my episodes. In addition to listening to healthy voices, one of the best things I did for myself was reading. Reading is one of the simplest but most powerful activities there is, and it completely changed my life. Immediately following my episodes, I still had difficulty with word-concept relationships, but as I continued to read I understood these better and it helped me to communicate better. Once I had the language to identify issues in my life, which can be the most difficult part of therapy, I was able to better work with these issues and overcome them. Reading developed my communication ability, it strengthened and solidified my internal monologue, it improved my short-term and long-term memory, and it improved my attention span.

Having the language to identify and work with concepts was extremely important for me because a great deal of my recovery happened in talk therapy and eventually on my own with journaling. I usually thought through my issues before coming to therapy, and the reason I was able to do this was mostly that I had done so much reading. Reading helped me to develop a strong internal monologue; I could retain thoughts for longer periods of time in order to analyze and work with them in my mind. Besides helping develop my short-term memory, that is, the ability to retain my thoughts, reading also increased my long-term memory. After having read for a while I began remembering things from my past which I had completely forgotten and which were essential for overcoming my illness. My once distant past was now visible and detailed and I was able to better work with the issues that were affecting me. I developed the ability to remember a traumatic experience, identify the issue associated with it, and then pacify the fears and worries I had surrounding it. Having the language to work with concepts enabled me to improve my thinking and improve my socialization skills. This eventually helped me to obtain most of my life goals and get to a point where I now consider myself living a happy and meaningful life.

Parent-Patient Interactions

During my schizoaffective disorder episodes and for a couple years following them my interactions with my parents were usually non-existent or discordant. The few times we actually talked were usually spent arguing, but I mostly isolated myself. During my childhood, I lived in a strict household where there was stern discipline and a lot of rules to follow. I was constantly being told what to do, whether it was cleaning my plate, working harder, keeping my fingers off the walls, taking my shoes off, helping with groceries, and everything else imaginable. Many of these directions were normal parental demands, but over time they began to wear on me. There were many times I knew the right thing to do but my parents kept telling me because they didn't trust that I would independently decide to do what I needed to. There was always someone telling me what to do. It felt very condescending and diminishing that no one thought I had the ability to figure out the right course of action by myself.

I grew up with a cognitive impairment and there were many times when people outside of my house gave me directions. Life was blurry in my mind when I was growing up; I had difficulty thinking with clarity, and the people around me knew it and constantly ordered me around. It got to the point in my teenage years where I usually relied upon other people to figure out what I should be doing and wasn't able to draw conclusions independently. Part of this was cognitive impairment but another part was seeking approval from others. I had a difficult middle school experience where I was constantly ridiculed for about a year and a half. After that I felt compelled to "fit in" whenever possible. Therefore, in later years I decided I had to do what others were doing and I unwittingly compromised my ability to think for myself just by trying to fit in.

While being disciplined from the earliest of ages my Dad always yelled and got in my face and intimidated me into believing what he wanted me to. Any time I tried talking back he yelled, "Don't you talk back to me! I'm your father and whatever I say goes!" This was very debilitating and after my middle school experience I found I was extremely afraid and completely unable to stand up for myself. In later years I attributed my inability to defend myself as a result of poor parenting. During and after my episodes I also drew the conclusion that my inability to stand up for myself was one of the many reasons I was so unhappy. Throughout my earlier life up until my second episode I had been constantly made fun of so standing up for myself was a salient issue. I became angry that my ability to defend myself had been taken away from me.

As my first episode began at age nineteen I wanted others to consider me smart and to treat me with respect. I had been constantly ridiculed for lacking intelligence in earlier years and it was painful when people made fun of me because it made me feel diminutive, alienated, and unintelligent. I also knew I had a cognitive impairment and was doing my best to be intelligent and fit in. My mind just wasn't developed enough and I also had the cognitive impairment which set me back. As my first episode developed so did my mental rigidity. My mental rigidity was centered around making precepts and a belief system that others would think was intelligent which was a result of the saliency of my difficult social experiences growing up. I thought once others respected me and thought I was intelligent all my problems would disappear and no one would ever make fun of me again. I hated being made fun of more than anything. There were also many personality quirks I had picked up from my parents that I began reflecting upon and decided were the main reason for having been made fun so much.

As my first episode progressed I began losing friends because I wouldn't allow people to make fun of me or disrespect me even the slightest bit. I wanted absolute respect from everyone and lost my ability to take a joke and joke back with others. As I was losing friends and became lonelier my episode worsened and I started searching for reasons I had become the way I was. I was also having difficulty with insomnia and exhaustion from mania and this didn't help my thinking. I looked back on my childhood and decided the reasons I had so much difficulty socially were entirely a result of the way my parents had brought me up. I determined there were many issues caused by my parents contributing to negative social interactions but they in fact were not the reasons for having had so much social difficulty. I blamed my Dad for being overly strict and yelling at me too much. I thought he was the reason I became unable to stand up for myself and was extremely angry at him for it. He has also usually been the butt of many jokes in our family and I blamed my emulation of his person-ality as the reason I became that same way which in part was true.

During and after episodes I was more willing to talk to my mom but I was still somewhat angry at her. She's very intelligent but is sometimes negative. In middle school, I blamed all the negativity I remembered having as a direct result of having spent time with her and having heard her be negative towards me. Some-times she just had difficulty being positive and she was occasionally negative but not nearly as much as I had perceived her to be. She also has depression and that was a part of it but the main reason I had picked up her negativity was from being so depressed myself. When I was depressed I had a repetition compulsion to look for depressing information and have depressing conversa-tions because I became so comfortable with melan-choly feelings.

At the start of my first episode I remembered all these things and completely isolated myself for about six months. I had been told so many different things from so many different people that I just decided I needed to be alone to figure life out. There were too many conflicting values being thrown at me and I just wanted some time alone to think for myself. I hated being told to do anything and whenever I was asked or told to do something by my parents I yelled over the phone at them as loud as I could and usually hung up afterwards. In my earlier years, I was also very impulsive and felt everyone other than myself was in control of my life and I sought to gain as much control over my life as I possibly could. Any time anyone even suggested something for me to do I went to great ends to ensure that it was something I decided to do. I would tell them no I won't do that, and then I would tell myself the same thing they had told me and proceed to do it. I was afraid of being controlled by any outside influences and whenever I thought someone was being controlling it really got under my skin and made me feel extremely awkward. I thought my inability to think for myself was one of the main reasons I had been made fun of so much and was a reason I was experiencing the episode which at the time I didn't know was an episode but just understood was an awful way to live.

I lost trust in anyone and everyone who had ever been a part of my life including my parents. I thought people were out to get me and I became increasingly more paranoid as my episode became a mental illness. By the end of the six to eight-month period where my illness was at its worst my parents intervened. I had difficulty talking with them. The one thing they told me that eventually made me listen to and get along with them again was that, "We are on your side and we want to help you. We care for you." Hearing these words was really important for me and encouraged me to listen to them. It helped them get me to the hospital and ultimately get me to a healthier state of being.

Although I was hospitalized and my health was improving there were still many issues between my parents and myself. Over the years, I realized I had expected perfection from them and didn't realize they were human and were learning from experience just as much as I was. My mom eventually told me she was being medicated for depression and this made me far more understanding of her previous negativity. Hearing that she had an ailment of her own made me more forgiving and allowed me to let go of the anger I had towards her from having thought she contributed to my negativity and depression during middle school. She still is very intelligent and is the parent I talk to the most about issues in my life.

My relationship with my Dad took a few years to rebuild. There were a couple years after my second episode where I barely spoke to him and I mostly blamed him for all the difficulties I had in my life. He wasn't as socially adept and intelligent as my Mom and I blamed him for not teaching me things and talking to me about social situations in more depth. I felt if he would have talked with me more about my problems instead of telling me I needed to toughen up I would have done much better. There had been many times where I mentioned a problem and he told me I needed to get tough, instead of just talk about the issue and figure it out the way I do now. This has been his nature throughout his life and I've learned that he has issues of his own but for some reason just doesn't like to talk about his problems. Knowing this has helped me forgive him more.

As I grew older my parents changed the way they treated me which gave me more respect for them. I was still living at home after my episodes and my par- ents let me decide what I would do and began treating me as an equal. Being treated this way was important because they were giving me the respect I had been looking for. They were also allowing me to make my own decisions and learn from experience which I was also grateful for. This made me feel I was at least competent enough to run my own life but also made me feel more respected for my intelligence and for my decision-making ability. I had been ridiculed for my intelligence as previously mentioned and being trusted with my own life made me feel I was capable of taking care of myself. One thing I had been angry about in earlier years and during episodes was not being allowed to make decisions for myself. Once I was allowed to do this it felt empowering and it made me feel I had more control over my life. I did in fact make some poor decisions but I learned from them and I was in the driver seat instead of the passenger seat. Having been in the passenger seat of my own life previously made me feel very helpless and gave me the notion I had no control or agency whatsoever. A part of the reason for the lack of agency and control over my life was because I hadn't developed the ability to determine the options of decisions and evaluate their consequences. This happened simply from having not done it much at all for so many years. I think if I was given more freedom during earlier years to make decisions I would have developed much better. The point is they were giving me this freedom after my episodes even though I still wasn't anywhere near having good mental health and this gave me more respect for them which in turn improved our relationship.

Another small facet of our interactions was not being judged for every little thing I had to say. Throughout my life up until after my second episode my words were constantly judged and ridiculed by others frequently, including my parents. When they became more accepting of what I had to say it made me feel better. Sometimes I swear when I'm around them or talk in different tones but when they just accept the way I want to talk and treat me the way they would any other adult I have found I have had far more respect for them than at any other time. We have also had far more to talk about and I have been more willing to accept their advice when I need to.

Once my mental health improved I eventually realized there were in fact many personality quirks I had gained from my parents but these weren't the reasons people had disliked me. I realized my parents have a lot of friends so having these quirks couldn't have made people dislike me. The main reason I had attributed their personality quirks as the reason for my mental illness was that I wanted someone to blame for the illness. For a while I thought if I can't blame myself I have to blame someone else and they seemed like the most viable option. As my mental health improved I came to understand I didn't do anything to create or cause my illness and no else had either. It was completely dumb luck that I was born with a cognitive impairment that developed into schizoaffective disorder and nothing anyone could have said or done could have prevented it. This made me realize I was wrongfully blaming my parents and I was very apologetic afterwards. I learned there were many issues they had no control over which were the main reasons for my having had such a difficult life and ironically enough it was their help that got me through some of the toughest situations I've ever faced. I also realized it was my parents' best qualities which helped me overcome my mental illness; those being intelligence, a will to do what's best, and a great work ethic. I currently look for peoples' best qualities and if I find them useful I'll strive to make them my own.

Auditory Hallucinations

Experiencing and Overcoming Schizoaffective Disorder

One day after work I was home alone and had been alone for some time and heard someone say "hey" to me and looked in the direction I heard the voice. The voice came from the door leading into the garage and no one was in our garage. Anything that could make noise was turned off and I realized it was my mind generating the voice. There have been several instances that this has happened and I have realized it mostly occurs when I am mentally exhausted and also while I'm stressed. I know the voices are not generated by my conscious mind but are heard by my conscious mind. They are always reverberations of things I have heard such as a song or a past voice from someone I have known. I have heard these sounds, songs, or voices from within my mind but it is not something I am consciously generating. I usually hear it from a direction that seems to be outside myself such as directly to my left or to my right or at a diagonal. This means it does not come from the area of my mind where I generate and hear my internal monologue. It always seems as though it's something I'm hearing outside of my conscious mind but not outside of my head. The hallucinations seem to linger somewhere in between internal and external. Sometimes they are very clear and other times there's a fuzziness to them which sounds like a TV on a very low volume does.

To alleviate this burden, I'll think about my surroundings and I'll determine if there is anyone or anything present which could have created the voice and if not then I've realized it was my subconscious. Once I am able to determine if it's a hallucination or not I decide whether it is or is not something I need to act upon. Hearing someone speak usually turns me towards that direction but obviously if no one is there then I know it's a hallucination. If I have a suspicion it's a hallucination and someone is there I'll usually ask if they just said something. Determining the sound is a hallucination informs me that my stress levels are really high and I need to do something to reduce them. Sometimes I'll take a day off from work if this occurs or just do something relaxing like eating a snack and watching something funny on TV.

I have never had an auditory hallucination with a creative element that was speaking directly to me. They have always been reiterations of things I have already heard.

Finding and Creating Yourself

From my middle school years all the way up to my first episode of schizoaffective disorder I had a difficult time with being made fun of and bullied. I was a good kid and usually did the right thing but I had a cognitive impairment, social anxiety, and difficulty standing up for myself. My middle school years created my social anxiety and inability to defend myself and these problems hampered me for years. One of the main reasons I developed so much mental rigidity leading into my first episode was because I disliked who I was from having been made fun of so much and was trying to become someone different. I had a personality disorder where I wasn't satisfied with who I was and also didn't know who I wanted to become. I had been constantly ridiculed for having a lack of intelligence, slow wit, and for being inarticulate in the years preceding my episodes and thought about how I could change this. I wanted to become someone who was intelligent and respected by everyone, but I was uncertain of how to do it. In the midst of my first episode I had become someone who had no friends and had no clue who he was but didn't know how to change. I was usually angry, had a chip on my shoulder, I was way too stringent, hated having fun, and was very mentally rigid. This happened because I attempted to change the way I was to fit in to become more popular. I had already been popular before I turned into the episodic person but I was unhappy with my life because of all the ridicule I had received and my inability to stand up for myself. Many people would say it's important to accept who you are, but this wasn't something that was working for me during the episode or before it. I had a nebulous vision of who I was and wasn't certain of who I wanted to be. I heard two contrasting ideals; "Life is about finding yourself," and "Life isn't about finding yourself; it's about creating yourself." In my social rehabilitation, I found I had to accept certain things about myself and determine what has been working, but I also had to change the things that haven't been working. I needed to create a different way of life and develop better socialization skills.

While redefining my personality I ran into a number of issues which negatively affected my mental health. I disliked my previous self and wanted to completely change everything I could. I didn't realize this simply isn't possible. I originally thought my problems were biological when in reality they were philosophical. I'm a high-energy guy who is very personable and jovial. Attempting to change my biology created a lot of physiological issues as well as social ones. For example, I thought I had too much energy and was too happy and tried decreasing my energy levels and putting myself into bad moods to try to fit in. Sometimes certain parts of my brain hurt while thinking certain things and other times I had heart pain. The first stage of my recovery in later years was allowing my mind and body to function the way they naturally do. I came to understand that those are things I am not capable of changing—but they are things I don't need to change to obtain what I want in life.

Socially I'm gregarious and tend to gravitate towards people, but during my first episode I tried to completely change this. I had always been a nice guy but I started being mean to people during and shortly after my episodes. I thought I had been made fun of for having too much fun and being too jovial in earlier years, so I decided I had to have something to be upset about all the time. I had to act like I was tough because that seemed to be the way of the people surrounding me. This created a lot of stress for me and strained my relationships. I became unable to functionally interact with others; I wouldn't allow anyone to make fun of me or joke with me even the slightest bit. I wanted to prove that I was an intelligent person who demanded respect. Being ridiculed had caused me a lot of emotional pain, so it was a major issue for me. I decided to work as much as I possibly could so I would constantly have some sort of adversity in my life that I could complain about. I wanted people to believe I was earning everything I owned because I had also been ridiculed for being affluent. I made my life more difficult simply because I wanted to be liked. I eventually learned there were many things about my younger self that were working really well and I reintegrated them into my life. I learned nice guys finish first and joviality is great and enjoyable. Some personality traits I had been trying to change had been working very well. I had all the tools to be a respectable, intelligent, and well-liked person but just needed to learn a few new things and develop some of my social skills. Accepting what has been working and adjusting what was not is how I developed a healthy personality.

The part of myself I did change however, was my knowledge base. After becoming an English major I learned that literature offered a lot of valuable wisdom that could help me improve as a person, and I began studying literature just to improve the quality of my social interactions. I began developing social skills just from reading and gained a better understanding of life. I began making better decisions than I had been in earlier years. Reading and thinking helped developed my mind and improved my thinking and articulation skills, which helped me socialize better. For the first twenty years of my life I hadn't thought much about life or really decided upon a direction for myself but simply thinking about life helped me figure this out. I eventually decided I wanted to be easy-going but also intelligent, and learned I could become this way just by making good decisions. I currently strive for mental flexibility and don't like to define myself too narrowly because I like having the ability to adjust and adapt to each situation's requirements.

Reading helped me develop agency and as I was able to live in the moment more I was able to more actively determine the path I wanted to take. Instead of acting impulsively I now thought out the consequences of my actions and made good decisions. There were times in earlier years where my impulsivity got me in trouble, but now I was thinking about cause and effect and consequences. There were times I still made mistakes but overall I made good decisions. I was redefining my self-image simply by making decisions that were scrupulous, conscientious, and intelligent, which lead to high functionality, and basically were demonstrative of the ways I wanted to be. Initially it was more difficult to break out of old habits but after making a good number of quality decisions it became more natural. I also began thinking of myself more in terms of the decisions I had made more recently, rather than ones I had made in younger years. My memory of these decisions redefined the way I viewed myself. Good decision making became much easier because I was in the habit, and my recollection of the good decisions I made was the information I drew from to make new decisions.

I also decided to start hanging out with people who were more respectful and had similar interests. This meant leaving behind old friends for people who were more respectful, kinder, and more intelligent. Surrounding myself with people who were smart and respectful improved my well-being, but also helped me determine how I wanted to be as a person. I could see the things that they did well and learned how to adopt good qualities from my new friends. In earlier years I had experienced difficulty from striving to be too much like my peers, but I eventually learned to view myself as neither different from or similar to anyone else. I have a creative mind and I simply like to evaluate a situation and decide what the best course of action is, regardless of who is or isn't doing it. It's helped me become an individual who is a part of the group — something I was striving for. Sometimes I'm the same as my peers and other times I'm completely different. I've developed some great friendships and learned that having good people in my life who care about me is far more important than being popular. I do like to make new friends and have as many friends as possible, but I understand if someone is disrespectful I don't need to deal with them simply for the sake of being liked.

There were other socially dysfunctional habits I had retained from my episodes that I also had to change. I felt compelled to repeat certain behaviors simply because I was afraid of change and because I was comfortable with habit. The repetition compulsion

(Freud) was difficult to overcome initially. I learned that when combatting a repetitive behavior, I have to first create a replacement behavior that I can practice during the same or similar situation to take the original behavior's stead. I realized I need to have the courage to at least try the new behavior and give it a fair chance. This was tough but became easier over time as I realized that I can always revert to the old behavior if the new one isn't working, or go back to the drawing board. Every behavior has an incentive and the way I undermined bad habits was by figuring out my incentive for them. Sometimes if I had difficulty changing a behavior I simply told myself the new behavior will help me gain the same incentive far better than the old one. I also informed myself the extent of the incentive will be greater. So when I had been practicing a problematic behavior and finally realized it, I drew up a new behavior and informed myself it would make me even happier than the original one, which usually was the case.

For example, although things were going well with my new friends I still had difficulty standing up for myself. During my episodes, I had become too angry while defending myself, but during the years previous to schizoaffective disorder I had acquiesced to everything everyone was saying. I found myself caught in between, but wasn't happy with disrespect. The other problem with allowing others to be disrespectful is that the more I've allowed it, the more comfortable they've felt behaving that way. While re-assimilating socially I learned I had to allow people to at least joke with me. I was afraid at first because I didn't want to become the butt of everyone's jokes; ridicule was painful. But I exposed myself to allowing others to joke with me. I had to tell myself "All friends joke with each other. I'll be happier allowing people to joke with me rather than being harsh and disrespectful when they do." I learned that if I allow friends to joke with me I can joke back, and I can still let people know when I have a problem with something they are saying. I eventually learned how to stand up for myself too. I decided I want to be jovial and lighthearted when standing up for myself, but still get my point across. This mind set helped me retain friends and have some laughs while still accomplishing the task of defending myself and retaining respect while not disrespecting anyone. If I never exposed myself to my fear I would have never developed a good technique for standing up for myself. Joking is an essential part of friendship and if I didn't allow others to joke I would probably not have made very many friends.

Over several years I developed and learned more socialization skills such as standing up for myself. I realized I didn't have to change the biological facets of my personality; I still have a lot of energy and I am very jovial. Acquiring new knowledge about socialization and developing new skills helped me resolve the issues that had led to my mental rigidity which had been inhibiting my social interactions. This led to an improvement in my socialization and helped me acquire several very good groups of friends who I still hang out with today.

Made in the USA
Lexington, KY
18 August 2018